O' Connor, C.

CHRISTY

CHRISTY O'CONNOR

Junior's

GOLF MASTERCLASS

Foreword by Christy O'Connor Senior

7/386409

CollinsWillow

An Imprint of HarperCollins*Publishers*

First published in 1993 by
Collins Willow
an imprint of HarperCollins Publishers
London

A CIP catalogue record for this book
is available from the British Library

ISBN 0 00 218520 2

Designed and produced by
MasterClass Design Ltd
37 Seymour Close, Birmingham B29 7JD
Photography by Mark Newcombe, Visions in Golf
Illustrations by MasterClass Design Studio
Colour origination by Colourscan, Singapore

Printed and bound in Portugal by
Printer Portuguesa-Sintra

CONTENTS

Foreword

BY

Christy O'Connor Senior

The late, great Bob Wallace was a very close and dear friend to the O'Connor clan from Knockmacarra. As the professional at the nearby Galway club this big, rotund man of great golfing wisdom gave me my first break in the game when I became his assistant in 1946.

They were amongst the happiest days of my life, learning the art of club-making, listening to his every word and practising and playing under his watchful, caring and kind eyes.

Twenty years later my nephew, Christy Junior, was to be found in Bob's shop, almost unchanged in two decades, listening to the same advice and learning the very same basics of this great game.

Christy Junior spent a year also as assistant to Bob's son, Kevin, when he became the professional at South Shields before returning to Ireland. Christy's elder brother Sean was my assistant at Royal Dublin, but had decided to take up an appointment in the Bahamas. I decided to take young Christy under my wing.

I had been privileged to gain the experience of twenty years on the world tournament circuit, including many Ryder Cup battles, and it was with great pride that I nurtured and enjoyed the progress of my young nephew.

Now, a further twenty-five years on, I can look back with immense pride in the manner in which Christy Junior has not only carried the name of O'Connor but has become Ireland's golfing ambassador to the world.

His success on the tournament circuit and in major events like the Ryder Cup comes from thousands of dedicated hours spent on the practice fairways, on the greens and in the bunkers, where he has honed his skills of shot choice and shot-making; and through his experience on the tournament scene the knowledge and ability to play the right shot at the right time in the heat of first-class competition.

KNOW YOUR CLUBS

It is a fact that at least 60% of the shots you play in a round of golf are played from within 100 yards of the pin, which is why the short game is so important and why, if you seriously want to improve your golf, you should spend more time practising this part of your game rather than trying to blast golf balls out of sight at the driving range.

In my experience, having played the European Tour and other events world-wide for almost a quarter of a century, during which time I have played in hundreds of pro-am tournaments, the average club golfer does not understand how best to use his or her clubs.

A set of clubs contains fourteen clubs, including the putter. There are, in a normal set of golf clubs, about ten irons and three woods – for now I shall put aside the putter as that is the only club everyone knows when to use, if not how, though even that has some uses you have probably never thought of.

The ten irons should, by definition, each be used for a different distance, yet I think the majority of golfers can only hit the ball about four or five different distances, thus virtually misusing half the set of clubs.

As they are not cheap this seems to me like an awful waste of money.

What you should do is to fully utilise every one of your clubs properly, thus getting the full value from your hefty investment. Otherwise, it seems a waste

It is a fact that 60% of the shots in golf are played from within 100 yards of the pin.

of money buying them as well as a waste of energy carrying all fourteen round the golf course.

Each club has a different loft on its face and should be used for a specific distance. Whilst everyone's distances vary, with professionals often being able to hit the ball greater distances than the club golfer, normally with better direction, in ideal conditions, on a warm summer's day with no wind to speak of and a firm, flat fairway, I normally use each of my irons for the following distances.

Club	From	To
Wedge	60	110
9	110	130
8	130	145
7	145	155
6	155	165
5	165	175
4	175	185
3	185	200
2	200	220

I would emphasise that these are my distances and if yours are different from these don't worry as it is more the gradual increase in distance for each club that is important. You must get to know your distances, and to check them every six weeks as the seasons change. Make a note of them in a little book and keep it in your golf bag.

Ladies normally do not hit the ball as far as men, though they are often more expert at the short game where a full, though slow swing is required.

Their average distances, again in ideal conditions, are as follows.

Club	From	To
Wedge	50	90
9	90	100
8	100	110
7	110	120
6	120	130
5	130	140
4	140	150
3	150	160

Get to know how far you hit each club so that you never have to worry about taking the right club.

I have not included a 2-iron for ladies as it is a club few of them carry. They tend to be better with the 5-wood and even the 7-wood, which is a very good club for a lady or a more senior golfer.

You must also remember that in cold or wet weather you will not hit the ball as far as on a warm summer's day. Rain-proof or warm clothing for winter also restricts your shoulder turn so you will never be able to hit as far. When the weather is cold or damp you will hit about ten to fifteen yards less.

That's at least another club.

A great many golfers of just average ability could probably out-hit me on these distances in the shorter clubs, but I know that once we get to the 4-iron I'll leave them standing.

The 2-iron I hit on the 18th at The Belfry in the 1989 Ryder Cup was a shot of 215 yards. It was a distance I knew I could hit with that club or I would not have tried it. You don't need to take unnecessary risks in golf, at any level. least of all that. As I stepped up to the ball I immediately saw the shot and had no hesitation in playing it with

A shot I shall never forget, with a 2-iron 215 yards to the 18th green at The Belfry.

that 2-iron. Had I seen it differently, with a 3-wood, or perhaps a 5-wood, that is what I would have taken. Although I cannot really teach you to 'see' shots, as that is something that only comes with experience, you will 'feel' a shot now and again and I would urge you to go for that particular shot. If you are confident of hitting it, you are halfway to achieving it.

But let's move back to the correct use of your clubs.

I doubt that many club golfers of average ability could regularly strike a 2-iron off the fairway to the distance I had at The Belfry.

Many club golfers can hit a 7-iron not much less distance than they normally hit a 4-iron, yet for me there's about a 30-yard difference. Why?

It is all down to understanding how to get your clubs to work for you, and then of having the technique to use them effectively.

In this book I am going to show you how to use your clubs to do the job for which they were designed.

There are certain fundamentals in golf that you must master. Basically these are the grip, stance and alignment. Your grip is of major importance and though I don't want to spend too much time on it, you should. Get your grip correct and golf becomes so much easier. It's like building a house. If you put in firm foundations the house will remain standing. If you start building

Your grip is vitally important if you are to become a competent golfer.

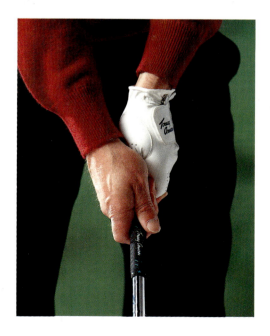

the walls on sand I don't think you'll get very far with it before it collapses around your ears. Golf is the same.

You probably already know that the club should sit across the left hand from the heel of the hand to the first joint on the index finger. Most people get this right. What a lot of them do is to grip it too high up the shaft. You must always leave about a half inch overlapping the edge of the left hand.

If you look at the gloves of many golfers you will see that there is a patch worn away at the heel of the hand. This is caused either by a bad grip, the club twisting in the hand as they swing, or, more likely, the fact that the top ridge of the club grip is rubbing because it is gripped too high.

Grip down a little, leaving a half inch showing all the time, possibly more. Gripping down does two things. First it stops your gloves wearing out quickly; and secondly it gives you more control in the hands.

Many golfers believe that if they grip down further they will lose distance. Yes, they will; which brings me back to my first point about not understanding what each club should be used for.

Before we leave the grip there are a couple of other things to check.

Although you hold the club more in the palm of your left hand, the right hand holds the club more towards the fingers. I always have the club laying across the base of the fingers of the right hand, where they join the top part of the palm.

The thumb pad of the right hand squeezes over the top of the left thumb as that extends a little down the shaft, though be careful not to push it down too far. You should be able to see one to two knuckles on your left hand as you look down, though ladies should grip a little more strongly and be able to see two to three knuckles. Your left thumb is slightly to the right of centre of the club shaft as you look down. You should feel the pressure in the ring and little finger of each hand, not the first and middle fingers so much.

Your stance is important too and I want you to avoid the slicer's grip and stance straight away. Take your grip as I have outlined and then look carefully at the position of your arms.

You may find that your right elbow is in front of your left, as you look down the line towards the target. If that's the case, pull it back straight away, getting it closer to your body. You almost feel that you are tucking it into the right side of the body.

Practise this little routine on taking your grip. Take your grip as normal, then, without altering your shoulder line, move your right hand off the grip and place it above the left. Look how that has pulled the right elbow in closer to the body. Your left elbow is held a little further forward than the right. That's how you want it.

Now, keeping that right elbow tucked in, move your right hand back to its proper position on the club. That will set you up with a professional grip and will make you hit the ball from an inside path, not slicing the ball but drawing it round left in the air, the way the professionals do. It's that easy!

Left handed golfers need to reverse these positions, with the grip laying across the right hand to begin with,

from the heel to the first joint of the index finger; the left hand fits over it with the club held at the point where the fingers join the palm.

The left hand holds the club more in the fingers, never in the palm.

Stand with your left elbow tucked more into the side of the body which will make you hit the ball from inside, turning it slightly left to right in the air, the ideal shape of shot.

Your alignment is very important as you must aim the club at your target. Beware of tee markers that are not

Keep your right arm tucked in at address or you will tend to slice the ball, your body comfortably poised.

square to the line of the fairway.

Find a small mark on the ground a couple of feet away from the ball as an intermediate target, aligning your club to that, your feet being parallel to that line for a straight shot.

Most golf shots demand a full swing. This means you really must turn your shoulders *fully* as you swing back in order to produce the wide arc you need to hit through the shot.

Even when you swing with a less-than-full swing, or swing slower, as in a bunker, for example, you must still turn

Pull down hard as though you were pulling on a bell rope.

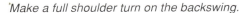

'Make a full shoulder turn on the backswing.

your shoulders right round. Get into the habit of really pulling them round, at least 90° to their original position at address. Never make a !azy half-turn.

From that full shoulder turn get the feeling that you are pulling down hard with both hands, as though you were pulling a church bell rope, as you turn your hips back through the ball. I shall be dealing with this subject in more detail later but get into the habit of always making a complete swing on a full shot.

The weight, which was about equal as you address the ball moves to the inside of the right heel as you swing back. Don't let it sway, though; it must stay fixed above the back of the ball. It is vital that the weight is transferred to the left and forward towards the target as you hit the ball.

Your right knee should be kicking and turning left, throwing your body weight onto the left side. Without this transfer of weight you are just hitting at the ball with your arms, getting no power into the shot.

Notice how the weight is transferring to the left side through impact, though the head stays still above the back of the ball.

At the finish the weight has fully transferred to the left, leaving you balanced and facing the target.

You must hit down into the back of the ball, especially on the short and medium irons. Hitting down gets the ball up, the loft on the clubface doing that rather than you having to think about it. Never try to scoop the ball into the air, always hit *down*.

Always take a divot; even on a 2-iron I take a divot, albeit a very shallow one, though it is longer then the one I might take with a 9-iron.

To help you hit down firmly the ball is best played from about the middle of your stance, though it can vary slightly, something I shall deal with as we look through the way to play each club.

The other vital point in our list of foundations is to follow through fully, rather than quitting on the shot, when the hands and club are slowing down as you approach the ball, in which case you are likely to push the shot straight right (straight left for left handers); or if you flick at the ball with a wristy action, the hands stopping but the clubhead continuing through impact, though not in the right direction.

That will lead to a pull or hook.

You must also avoid the cricket shot, the hands continuing through but the club stopping at the ball.

Remember to swing fully, turning those shoulders right back, to hit down and to keep going, right through to the top, as if you were trying to hit another ball suspended at about waist high in front of you on the target line.

Remember, you have not hit the shot fully until you have swung through into the finish position. Never quit on the shot but continue right through.

A view of the finish looking towards the target. Someone standing behind you should see you like this.

SWING FAULTS

Before we move on to the use of your clubs I do just want to warn you about a couple of faults that I see all too often in club golfers, and in some players I partner in pro-ams around the world.

One major problem is that of picking the club up too quickly on the backswing. You can see this clearly in the photograph below and it is a fault you must avoid. Swing the club back low

Avoid swaying back too far. You must keep your head above the back of the ball.

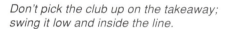

Don't pick the club up on the takeaway; swing it low and inside the line.

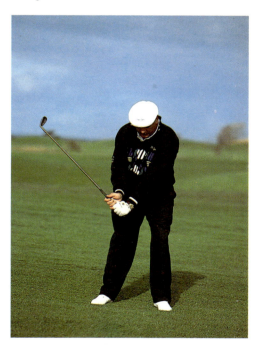

and inside the line, to build more width in your swing arc.

I have stressed, and will repeat throughout this book, how important it is to turn fully in the backswing. Your shoulders must turn fully but you must keep your head above the ball, one eye focused on the ball.

I see a lot of golfers sway on the backswing. That will pull you out of position and make it impossible to return the clubface square to the ball at impact. You will probably slice the ball.

Another major fault that many golfers

have is that of swaying in the opposite direction on the backswing; a reverse pivot. Once again this will pull you completely out of position and leave you no chance of hitting a good golf shot. You then have to move your arms incorrectly in an attempt to get the clubhead back square to the ball at impact.

One further fault at impact that I often see is that of falling back as you hit the ball, often in an attempt to get the ball higher in the air. The effect of this falling back is going to be exactly the opposite with you just topping the ball and keeping it lower.

Above right: *A reverse pivot occurs when you lean the other way on the backswing, again moving your body out of position.*

Right: *You must also avoid falling back as you come into the impact zone. That will only make you top the ball.*

USING YOUR CLUBS

From these foundations, back to the proper use of each club. From the wedge to the 5-iron I am looking for deadly accuracy, not distance for its own sake. Rather than hit an 8-iron flat out, straining every muscle to get the ball just on the green, I'll play an easy 7-iron, knowing that it will carry the distance I want and, more importantly, that I can control its direction and have it sit down on the green almost exactly where I want it to go.

There's nothing clever about being the longest hitter of an 8-iron on the course. You're better off taking a 7-iron, which is why you bought the thing in the first place.

With a wedge, or any other short iron, grip down the club for extra control, set the ball slightly back of centre of a fairly narrow stance, and have your hands slightly ahead of the ball.

Wedge

The ball should be slightly back of centre in your stance, which should not be too wide. Your knees should be comfortably flexed and I suggest you stand very slightly open to the target for this club, probably about 2–4 inches to the left of target.

Make sure, though, that your clubface *and your shoulders* are square to the target. At address your hands should be slightly ahead of the ball, with your weight slightly favouring your left side, about 60%.

Grip down about a half inch on the club as this gives you extra control.

The wedge is used for anything between about 60 and 110 yards so you need to vary the length of your back swing, though even at the maximum distance I would never wish to take more than a three-quarters swing with this club.

Remember, it is meant for pinpoint accuracy, not distance. If the shot you have means you have to hit it flat out, put it back in the bag and take out the

9-iron, which will allow you to hit the ball the correct distance without having to hit flat out.

Most professionals carry two or three wedges, but the standard wedge has a loft of 52°. It is ideal for shots of around 100 yards when, with a slightly open stance and a firm, downward strike into the back of the ball, you will get the backspin you require to stop the ball. That will only happen, though, if you hit the ball up into the air, or rather, let the club hit the ball up into the air. The loft on the clubface will do that quite easily so never try to hit it

Let the club get the ball airborne. Never try to scoop it.

upwards. Always hit downwards into the back of the ball. The club hits the ball before it reaches the bottom of its swing arc, which is why you take a divot.

Professionals use balata balls, which have softer covers than the surlyn balls, so will spin back better. If you are using a surlyn ball aim it to land at 94 yards, allowing it to run on very slightly to close to the pin.

One of the most valuable things around the green is knowing where you want to putt from, and this is what we spend so much time looking at during a practice round before a tournament.

If possible, you always want to leave yourself an uphill putt, particularly on fast greens where a downhill putt can just run away from you.

On your home course you will get to know the greens well, and will be aware of where the pin is normally placed. As you walk past greens that you will be playing to later in your round take a quick look to see where the pin is.

9-iron

Again, grip down a little to give you extra control as this is an iron to use for accuracy, not distance. Stand with your feet open about two inches but your shoulders parallel to the target.

Although you are seeking accuracy never try to guide the club as it goes through or your weight might fall back onto the right foot at impact and you will pull the ball left or hit it with more topspin rather than backspin. If you are swinging properly the club will go through on the correct plane.

8-iron

Stand about two inches open to the target, a stance you now keep for the remainder of the irons, but remember to keep your shoulders square to the target or you will be pulling the club across the ball and slicing it to varying degrees. The reason for standing very slightly open is to allow the hips to turn out of the way better on the downswing, giving you the freedom of space to swing the arms and club through fully without hindrance. If there is not enough space for the arms to swing down you risk blocking the shot and hitting the ball straight right.

The ball is also, from now on, slightly further forward in your stance, about level with the inside of your left heel.

The 8-iron is still a club for 100% accuracy rather than distance so never try to overhit it.

For the short irons I am looking for pinpoint accuracy, not distance. Stand slightly open and hit through the ball, transferring the weight to the left in a full finish.

7-iron – 6-iron – 5-iron

I shall deal with these together as they have the same purpose, though for slightly different distances. You should not be trying to hit harder with any one of them as it is the length of the shaft which, by producing a wider swing arc and thus more clubhead speed at impact, together with their gradually decreasing lofts, hits the ball further. The further the ball goes, the lower its trajectory.

With these clubs set up just the same, an inch open but with your shoulders parallel to the target line. You are still looking for accuracy rather than just distance for its own sake, so make a full swing, getting the shoulders right the way round and turning the body weight to the left side as you pull the club through impact.

The weight transfer is very important and you can help it by making sure your right knee turns to the left as you swing down. Many golfers kick that right knee out in front of them, which causes a loss of momentum in the swing.

Kick it to the left, so that you finish with your body facing the target or just slightly left of it and your right foot on tip-toe. It is very important to continue hitting through the ball, something I shall come back to later, but never stop swinging as soon as you have struck the ball. Make a full swing.

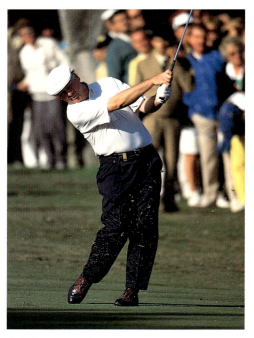

It is important that the right knee kicks left as you swing through impact. Make sure that knee turns to the left rather than kicking out in front of you.

4-iron – 3-iron – 2-iron

Now we are looking for distance and although you want to be as accurate as possible your aim should be to get the ball a sufficient distance that it finishes green-high, if not pin-high. Don't look for too much from the long irons in the way of pinpoint accuracy, as you should be aiming to reach a general area rather than a specific blade of grass.

Although you are looking for more

distance you must make a smooth, slow backswing, keeping the clubhead low to the ground on the takeaway as you want to sweep through the ball rather than slashing at it.

Never snatch at the backswing; the club comes to a complete stop at the top so there's little point in having a fast backswing.

You must remember the bell-rope analogy from a little earlier, pulling down hard with the hands and hit through the impact zone to that second ball suspended in front of you.

The power is driven by the weight transfer and as your feet are your only contact with the ground you can see how important good leg action is in driving the swing.

From a full shoulder turn your right leg will drive your weight to your left side, turning as you do so.

Even though you are hitting a long iron now, never be tempted to try to hit the ball up – hit it forwards, sweeping it off the grass. With the short irons you take a deep but short divot; with the long irons you take a shallow, but longer divot, the change being gradual from the wedge to the 2-iron.

On a 4-iron, for example, you should be taking a divot about a quarter of an inch deep and four inches long.

There are a few points I want to emphasise about the use of the irons before we move on. Never pick the club

With a long iron you are looking for distance so the legs must really drive the weight through the shot, transferring totally to the left at the finish.

up on the takeaway – always swing it low to the ground for the first couple of feet, keeping your left arm fairly straight, though natural. Never jerk the club back up steeply; let it swing in a circle as that will create a wider swing arc and thus more power and control.

At address hover the club just off the ground rather than grounding it. That will help you to make a smoother take-away by turning the left shoulder back. Never lean on the club, pressing it down just before you begin the take-away as that will take the feeling out of the shot as well as making you pick the club up too steeply with your wrists rather than swinging it back in a full, low arc.

Keep the left arm and the wrists held firm on the backswing until at least about waist height. The wrists will then cock of their own accord so you need never worry about cocking the wrists.

Even when you reach waist height, still keep swinging the club rather than trying to do anything different with it.

It must swing in a wide circle – let it! Don't force it out further, nor pull it inside. Let it flow naturally.

Your weight, as you get towards the top of the backswing, will be on the inside of your right heel and should stay there as the left shoulder turns fully so that it is under the chin. At the top of the backswing the club shaft should be horizontal and pointing parallel to the target line.

Never sway on the backswing – keep your weight firmly on the inside of your right foot and more towards the heel.

From a square set-up swing the club back low and slow on the inside.

Get a full shoulder turn, your left shoulder well under your chin.

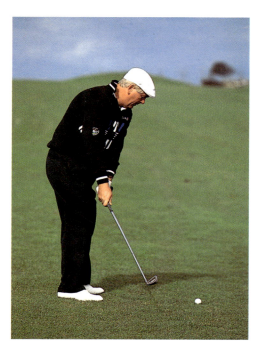

You must beware here, too, of the dreaded reverse pivot which is fatal to your swing. It happens if, as you swing the club back, your head and thus your body weight, moves left, ahead of the ball. Your head stays *behind* the ball at all times.

The first movement on the downswing is of the legs moving left, the left leg becoming a brace to hit against. Although the hips move laterally on the downswing you must not let your left leg sway forwards toward the target. Keep it firm, as you did the right leg on the backswing. You must avoid 'casting' on the downswing.

You will remember that I told you a little earlier to hold your right elbow in closer to your body at address to help create a stroke from inside. The same applies on the downswing. Keep that right arm tucked in closer to the body rather than letting it fly outwards, taking the club with it.

Your head is still behind the ball as you throw the club at and through the impact zone. Never have the feeling that you are hitting the ball and that's

As you come down to the impact position your weight begins to transfer to the left.

Continue through to a full finish, turning to face your target.

that – you must keep hitting through to that imaginary ball suspended at waist height. If you fail to finish in the high position you see professionals adopt, you will have begun decelerating the club before you reached the ball, thus robbing you of power and direction.

Many golfers have trouble getting the right distance from the ball at address. If you stand too close to the ball you will have to have an upright swing to get the clubhead back to the ball. A very upright swing is difficult to control and you will probably slice the ball.

Standing too far from the ball conversely causes a flatter swing, leading to you having to cast at the ball on the way down which will result in a hook.

The best way to judge the distance,

Always finish facing your target, or just left of it, your body balanced with your weight left.

which increases with the length of each club, is to take your address position and then let the very top of your club rest on your leg. It should be about four inches above the knee as a rough guide.

THE WOODS

I want, now, to move onto the woods and I shall start with the fairway woods, though I must emphasise that you can use them from other parts of the course as well, not just from a flat fairway.

5-wood

This is possibly the friendliest club in the bag, a really magnificent and versatile tool. You can use it to manufacture shots from anything between about 175 and 220 yards. It's a club you really must get to know well, by continually using it and practising with it.

It has about the same loft as a 4-iron and will hit a similar shape shot, though it can be used for a shot longer than a normal 4-iron.

If you have a 4-iron distance but you need extra height on the ball to carry a hazard in front of the green, for example, the 5-wood is the club to use. You can turn a difficult 4-iron shot into an easy 5-wood shot.

You can use it on the tee of a short par-3, from the rough, from sloping or hanging lies, from situations where the ball is in a divot, or from situations where you need its loft (to get over a tree, for example) as well as needing a reasonable distance, gripping down the shaft as necessary.

It really is one of the most useful clubs in your bag but you must remember to

always swing it with a very smooth, free rhythm, never trying to hit it further than it wants to go.

3-wood

This club I use from about 200 to 230 yards but one of the main reasons it is an enemy of the average golfer is that he tries to hit the ball up rather than sweeping it off the fairway. If you try to hit the ball on the upswing you will have pushed your weight backwards in relation to the target, taking all the power out of the shot.

A great practice tip is to place two tees in the ground, one where the ball should be, a second five inches nearer the target. Swing to hit the first tee but also keep the clubhead low enough that

The 5-wood is a wonderfully versatile club. As well as giving you good distance you can play it from rough, but make sure you do really hit through it smoothly, letting the club do the work.

The 3-wood is ideal for long fairway shots, or for use from the tee on tight driving holes, but you must fully turn your shoulders on the backswing.

it knocks the second tee-peg out of the ground as well. You can practise this in your garden as you don't need a ball.

This will teach you to follow through correctly, allowing the club to do the job it was designed for.

It is also excellent out of light rough when the ball is sitting up nicely, though never use it in heavy rough.

The Driver

I suggest that you do not use this club until you have been playing golf for at

Address the ball just inside your left heel.

least a full year. It has a very straight face and scares many golfers. It is, though, the club to use for the accomplished golfer as it will get him, or her, the greatest distance down the fairway.

Buying the right driver is important and I would never recommend that you buy a wooden headed driver with less than 12° loft, nor a metal-headed driver with less than 10° loft. I use a metal headed driver with 10° of loft.

One of the problems with this club is that most people think they have to hit the ball upwards off the tee. This is wrong. If you try to hit the ball up you will be hitting rather stiff-legged as you attempt to get the clubhead under the ball, rather than swinging through it.

As with the little practice tip with the 3-wood a moment ago, you should sweep through the ball to another tee-peg five inches further forwards. If you try to hit the ball upwards you will fall backwards.

Don't have the ball too far forward in your stance, no further forward than inside the left heel.

Although you are looking for maximum distance with the driver you must still swing within yourself, looking to hit the ball where you can see it, not hit it out of sight.

Opposite page: *There is sufficient loft on the clubface to get it airborne. Hit **through** the ball.*

PLAYING IN WINDY CONDITIONS

I grew up in Galway on the west coast of Ireland, a coast that is exposed to the full force of the winds rushing in from the Atlantic Ocean, quite often bringing rain squalls with them as well.

Playing golf in such conditions you have to learn to make a friend of the wind, using it to your advantage. It is pointless trying to fight the wind, as you'll never win.

There are, in fact, very few days on which there is no wind at all. You need to discover which direction the wind is blowing from, and how strong it is.

Always try to test the wind strength around you when you are about to take your shot, but don't forget to try to discover how hard the wind is blowing both at your target, whether that is the green or some other spot, and on the route to it.

You will often find that, particularly with a high pitch to the green there will be very little wind at ground level, both where you are and on the green, but if you look at the tops of trees on the course, at the height the ball will reach, there might well be a stiff breeze blowing. That is likely to affect the flight of the ball.

Always look at the flag on the green, any other flags there may be around the course and at the tops of trees. The other indicators of wind are the clouds, particularly low clouds. They never lie.

The other way the professionals test

There are certain places where the wind almost always blows, as on this exposed tee on my new course in Galway. Playing in the wind requires skill and patience.

the wind is by holding a few blades of grass at about shoulder level and letting them be carried away by the wind. This will tell you the wind speed and its direction.

Be extra careful on tree-lined courses for the wind can be funnelled and may seem to be blowing from a different direction to that which it really is.

Cross winds

I am going to to show you how to play particular lengths of shot in cross winds as well as into the wind and downwind. I shall begin with the most difficult wind for a right handed player, that blowing from left to right.

It might seem that the best shot would be one aimed left to begin with, to come round on the wind, but this is not the case. On a short shot (up to about a 6-iron in length) you must draw the ball into the wind, allowing it to hold against the wind so that it keeps on a nearly straight line.

Into a left to right wind you must take one club more than you think, at least. The general rule is that a 10 mph wind takes 10 yards off a shot, so always allow for this.

Aim just to the left of the pin but stand very slightly closed. You need to hit a good in-to-out shot, attacking the ball from inside the line, and you need a very pronounced follow through on a full swing.

I have said earlier that you must really turn your shoulders on the backswing. Into this wind you must also go right through the ball, almost exaggerating the follow through to get to the position that you see top professionals in as they finish a drive.

But don't strain to hit it harder – just swing within your own capabilities and at the same pace. Trying to swing faster in the wind is fatal as you will lose your balance and will probably end up mis-hitting the shot.

I do suggest you have a slightly stronger grip in a left to right wind, showing one knuckle more on your left hand as you look down.

On a long shot into the left to right wind you must use the wind to your advantage, starting the ball well left of target so that the wind will bring it round on target. Again I would suggest you take one club more as the wind will slow the ball down early in its flight.

In a strong left to right wind you will have trouble stopping the ball on the green if you are hitting a long shot, so take this into account in setting your target. If, for example, there is trouble on the right side of the green and you are hitting a long shot, try to leave it a little short so that, if it rolls as it inevitably will, it will still finish on the green and not off it to the right.

A right to left wind is easier for you should nearly always be looking to draw the ball, hitting a natural right to left shot, so it will carry on the wind.

As this shape of shot always travels further than one hit straight, or faded, it will run more on landing so always take one club less than you normally need for this distance.

When hitting a short approach to the green in a right to left wind, take one more club than normal and work the ball back into the wind, using the wind to control the ball, stopping it exactly where you want it.

By opening your stance a little and cutting the ball you will hit it higher but shorter, hence the extra club. The amount of sidespin on the ball will stop it very quickly once it lands.

Now for shots directly into the wind,

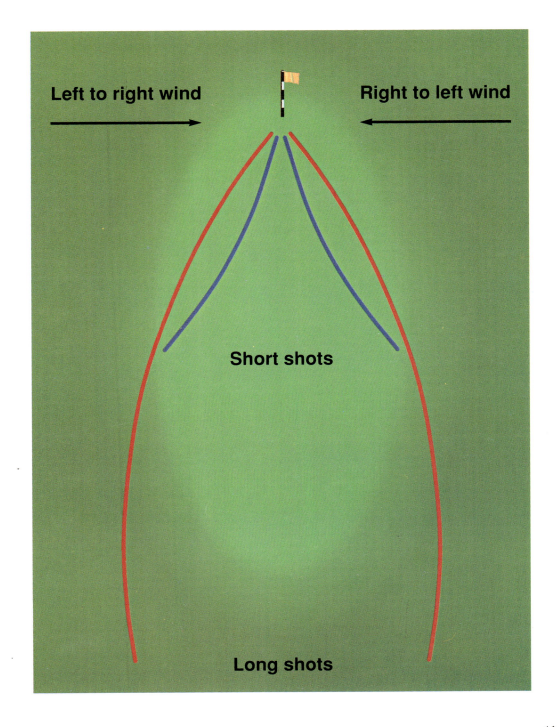

Left to right wind

Right to left wind

Short shots

Long shots

and these, like cross winds, cause the average golfer so much trouble, mainly because he tries to hit harder into the wind, disrupting his rhythm.

It is a misconception that you have to hit harder into the wind. Trying to overswing will throw you off-balance.

I will deal first with all shots apart from the driver.

Into the wind play the ball further back in your stance, about halfway between the centre of your stance and the back foot. Grip down the club about two or three inches to get more control over the clubhead. This forces you into making a stiffer wristed swing, not using the hands so much. Too much hand action into the wind can cause you problems.

Take a three-quarter swing, being very careful not to sway as you swing back. It might help you to stand with your feet slightly wider apart than usual, to help you keep your balance better.

Take a three-quarter swing keeping your wrists and hands firmer as you

Into a headwind make sure you stand very slightly closed and take only a three-quarters swing . . .

. . . and punch through the ball, finishing with the hands held out directly in front of you.

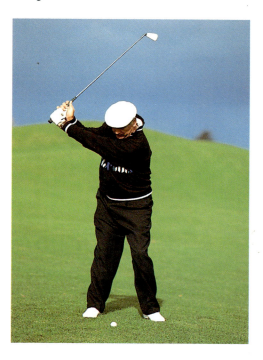

come through the ball, rather than letting them release as you normally do. The idea is to prevent the right hand rotating over the top of the left one after impact. You should finish with both arms out in front of you fairly straight, the back of the left hand still pointing towards the sky, the back of the right hand still pointing to the ground. The hands do come round the body a little, finishing to the left.

As you come into the hitting zone try to have the feeling that you have to hit two golf balls – the one on the ground and a second a few inches further on but beneath the ground very slightly. Punch down and through. Your weight should be on your left side throughout this shot.

Incidentally, although we shall come to the subject in detail later, you use virtually the same shot to keep the ball low under the overhanging branches of a tree.

Although the ball is staying lower on this shot, and will therefore run more on landing, you will probably need one more club because of the wind.

Note how the hands have not released. The right hand has not rotated over the left as it normally does.

The Driver

Now for the driver into the wind. Some of the tournaments we play are renowned for wind and you can always tell when conditions are bad because the scores go up fairly dramatically.

In the pro-ams the day before the tournament begins a strong headwind is the one thing that really shows up the golfers who are not accustomed to playing on anything but a calm day.

Tee the ball as usual. I have seen so many things in golf books and magazines telling people to tee higher, or tee lower. I don't do either. I tee as I would for every other drive.

The difference I make is in the way the driver contacts the ball for, instead of hitting it square on, I hit the ball halfway up, the bottom of the driver striking the middle of the ball. Some players think this is thinning the ball but it is not. It is driving the ball forwards on a low trajectory, but if you achieve good clubhead speed at impact you will hit the ball as far as on a calm day. Don't swing faster, though.

Your hands still drive down and through as in our previous shot. You must not try to hit the ball up as the spin on the ball and the loft on the clubface will do that. If you do try to hit it up you will thin it. That drives the ball down into the ground, taking all the sting out of the shot.

To help you hit it halfway up hover the clubhead off the ground at address rather than resting it on the ground as you might do now.

You can restrict your backswing a fraction if the wind is blowing hard. You should try to keep your balance comfortably and never swing faster than normal. If anything try to swing slower than normal and I am certain you will hit the ball better.

Downwind

Downwind shots are much easier, and I shall start with a tee-shot. This is the one occasion when I would definitely suggest you put aside the driver and reach for the 3-wood as the extra loft on the 3-wood (about 15° to the

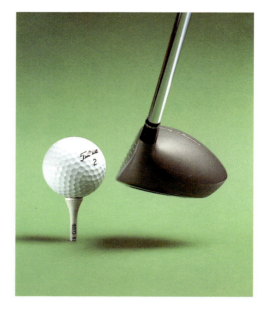

You can see here that I hit the ball halfway up, rather than full on.

driver's 10°) will hit the ball higher, allowing the wind to catch it and carry it further.

Tee the ball fairly low so that you sweep through the lower half of the ball, not trying to hit it higher but, once again, sweeping through the ball, keeping the clubhead low.

A lot of golfers think that, because they have a strong wind behind them blowing the ball towards the hole, that they need to take less club on a short shot. This is not so. Take the same club you would normally use for that distance, and grip down the club a little further than normal.

That gives you more control but will stiffen the wrists through impact, which will lead to a firmer downward strike into the ball. That is what gets the ball up with extra backspin, will bring it down and stop it without much run. It really does work.

You should practise sometimes in windy conditions, so that you learn to understand how the ball reacts, and also how the distances you hit the ball change from calm conditions.

You will often find that you need two clubs extra in either cross winds or directly into the wind. Only by practising in these conditions will you come to understand how to play these shots.

I now want to move on to some of the situations you will encounter on the course from time to time and to show you how to play them.

We all know that, on the practice ground, when there is no pressure because we know that if we hit a bad shot it really doesn't matter, when we are under pressure in a round of golf, particularly when you are playing for a major title or to see who buys the beer (probably more important!), there is only one chance to hit the shot. You have to get it right first.

When you are driving into a headwind avoid the temptation to swing faster. Just swing smoother.

ON THE TEE

The tee shot is one of the most important in golf, and nothing sounds, or looks, better than a well-struck drive flying down the middle of the fairway. A good drive sets you up for that particular hole and I seriously believe you should pay careful attention to getting your drives as long and straight as you possibly can.

Although you will not need a driver for every tee shot I am going to begin this chapter by telling you how to use the driver.

The driver is one of the loveliest clubs in the golf bag, as well as being a very individual club, yet I see so many people just buy one without thinking about what it will be used for, often buying one for its looks rather than its capabilities. Drivers these days come with coloured shafts, different size heads and are made of a variety of materials.

Getting one that suits you and your swing is not something to be taken lightly. I strongly urge you to go along to your club professional and ask him to select a club that will match your physique and swing rhythm.

I select a driver that is perfectly matched to my swing and I look for a number of different things before I buy.

The whippiness of the shaft, the swing weight and dead weight, which are all affected by your swing speed; the head size, whether the head is toed in very slightly, as many are these days, is square or open; the loft on the face,

A well struck drive not only looks and sounds good – it sets you up for that hole.

which can vary from about 8.5° to around 12°; the grip thickness, the length of the shaft, shaft material; all are things I look for and there is no reason why you should not do the same. Your professional has the expertise to advise you on the right driver for you, so don't buy something that just looks good but might not suit you.

Many golfers, I know, have beautiful drivers that sit quietly in the cupboard doing nothing, because they have been bought, tried once or twice with a minimum of success and then put away whilst either a 3-wood or another driver is used.

Whilst beginners to golf should use only a 3-wood off the tee for at least their first full year at the sport, to get into the habit of looking down at the face of a wood, a driver should be used if you want to really develop your long game and lower your scores.

The 3-wood, having more loft, will hit the ball higher off the tee so I think it is a good idea to use it at first. Yet the driver has plenty of loft to get the ball airborne. Indeed, many of us professionals use it regularly from the fairway when we have a very long shot.

My uncle, Christy Snr, was an expert with the driver off the fairway and in the days when he was playing on the Tour the drivers were all very square faced, not slightly closed or toed in, as they are today, to help you keep the ball straight.

At the practice ground you should really try to hit the driver from the fairway, off a decent lie, to give yourself extra confidence with this club.

Get into the habit of sweeping through the ball, something I shall come back to in a moment.

I tee the ball fairly high for a drive, something like one-and-a-half inches off the ground, the driver addressing the ball square on.

You will see that most professionals tend to stand very tentatively closed for the driver, with the left foot turned out

I normally tee the ball about one-and-a-half inches high, which is the depth shown here.

slightly towards the target. The ball is situated just inside the left heel. The closed stance helps to promote a good inside take away and a longer, fuller backswing. On this full shot you really must get your shoulders right round. You must make a very full shoulder turn as you swing back, getting as much width in the swing arc as you can, the left arm comfortably straight at the top of the backswing.

The main problem club golfers have in using the driver is that they slice the ball. They do this primarily because they try to get under the ball in an attempt to hit it up. In doing that the right shoulder gets outside the target line so the only way the club can hit the ball is from the outside, cutting across it and causing a slice. Try to keep that right shoulder inside the target line, Left handed golfers must keep their left shoulder inside.

With the driver you do not have to hit it up. It is sitting up already, on the little wooden tee-peg. All you need do is hit it forward.

One little tip from the tour is that, when we address the ball on the tee-peg, we make sure the number of the ball is on the right as we look down, so that it is at the back of the ball and just on the inside. That way you are trying to hit the number and if you have it positioned correctly you will be hitting straight up the back of the ball from the inside, a natural draw path. This will give you about an extra 15 yards on the shot, which is always welcome.

As you address the ball on the tee try to place it so that the number is on the right as you look down. Hit that with the club and you will have the correct swing pattern.

To help you with extra distance, and direction, show perhaps one more knuckle on your left hand at address, so that you are gripping very slightly stronger with that hand. That should also help to prevent you from fading the ball too much.

You must also avoid trying to flick the ball up into the air with your hands. I have said that the loft on the driver face is sufficient to get the ball airborne so you do not have to do anything more to it than hit it straight on as I have just described. Don't try to hit it up, just hit it forward.

You often see players hit the ball off the tee with the driver only to see it dip very quickly. This is because they have tried to hit it up rather than straight, and have topped or smothered it – hitting the ball downwards into the ground first. They then say that they can hit their 3-wood so much better and revert to that.

Well, of course, they can hit the 3-wood better because it has more loft on it and they are confident that the lofted face will get the ball airborne, so they concentrate on hitting the ball forward rather than up. If they were to transfer that same confidence to the loft of the driver they would find they would hit that up into the air well, also.

Finally, make sure that you hit through the ball with a sweeping motion, the clubhead still accelerating as you pass the impact zone and with your weight fully transferring to your left side to enable you to finish well balanced.

This is a full shot and there is no sweeter sound in golf than a perfectly hit shot leaving the driver face.

A brief word here about your tee shot itself. You will often get onto the first tee without having warmed up properly and in those circumstances you might be better taking a 3-wood for that shot, though I hope you will have the good sense to spend a half hour warming up and grooving the swing for that day.

We all suffer first tee nerves, at any level of golf and my advice to you is to 'see' the shot first in your mind's eye before you step up to address the ball.

Really be able to visualise where it is going to fly and where it will land, and have with you the shape of shots you have just been hitting on the practice ground.

You will feel your muscles tighten on that first tee, especially if you have the normal crowd standing close by watching you. Relax by talking to yourself, reminding yourself that you have just been hitting practice shots and keeping the same rhythm and swing thoughts that you had just a few minutes before. Do nothing different.

Keep your eye on the ball, swing slower rather than faster and make sure you turn fully on the backswing and then follow through completely, hitting through the ball and on into a good finish. Out on the course never tinker with your swing, but keep your same swing rhythm at all times. The place to adjust your swing is on the practice ground, not the golf course.

From a slightly closed address position, the ball positioned inside the left heel, the takeaway is slow and low.

The club is taken away low and long (top left) to the top of the backswing (top right). The knees then begin to transfer the weight (middle left) and the wrists are still cocked on the way down, the hands pulling down hard on the club (middle right). Just after impact (bottom left) and then the weight continues to transfer up into a full finish, (bottom right) my body facing the target 270 yards away, straight across the bay to the left of the bunkers.

Some more photographs of the driving sequence. Address the ball inside your left heel (top left) and take the club away smoothly and low to begin with. Again, you can see how straight the left arm stays on the way back (top right). At the top of the backswing (left) the shoulders have turned fully through 90°, my back at this point facing the target.

From the top of the backswing my hands begin pulling down very hard, as if I was pulling a bell rope (top left). My knees have already begun the weight transfer to my left side. This continues (top right) as my hands are still pulling the club down but now that I am approaching impact the hands are working hard to bring the clubface back square at impact. After impact the weight continues to transfer to the left (bottom right) showing that I have not quit on the shot but have hit right through it.

PAR-3 TEE SHOTS

It is well known, on Tour, that if any player pars all the par-3s – and there are normally four of them – he is going to end up with a very good score.

Par-3s are built to be tricky – it is part of the course designer's art to make them that way. Large bunkers, lakes and other hazards are all designed and situated to make you attempt to reach the green in one shot. Often a tricky pin position will tempt you to go for the flag rather than playing for the fat of the green.

If, for example, you have a par-3 with a pin cut in a tight position on the right of the green, but there is a large amount of green on the left, the most sensible shot is to go for the left side, where you have the biggest margin of error if you don't hit the shot perfectly.

That has happened so often. I have seen Nick Price win the 1993 TPC tournament at Sawgrass by playing the famous 17th sensibly, hitting a 9-iron to the heart of the green rather than going for the pin which his opponent on that day, Greg Norman attempted. Sadly, because Greg had to make up strokes he

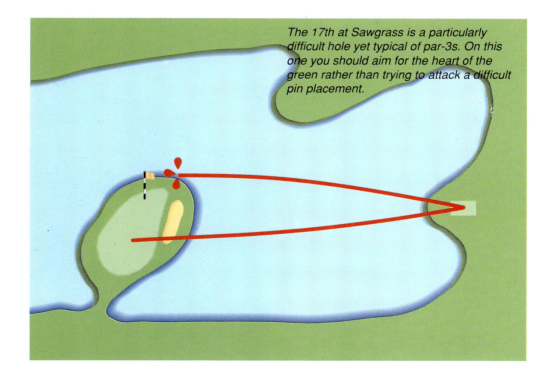

The 17th at Sawgrass is a particularly difficult hole yet typical of par-3s. On this one you should aim for the heart of the green rather than trying to attack a difficult pin placement.

had to take risks and his ball fell into the lake, leaving Nick Price with an easy two-putt par. That probably cost Greg the chance of a playoff.

That is the sort of thinking you should employ as well, not going for broke every time but playing sensibly and within your own limits.

The other thing to watch for on par-3s, is the exact distance to the pin, or to the heart of the green if you do not have the precise pin locations which we are given on Tour.

Always look very carefully at where the tee marker is set. The distance on the card may say 180 yards but the tee markers may have been moved forward 30 yards, so you might only be playing from 150 yards making up to three clubs' difference.

There is nothing to stop you pacing out the difference, so that you know how far you have to go, whether to hit the centre of the green or to avoid any bunkers or other hazards there may be just short of the green.

You are often better off hitting long, though nowadays many par-3s are being constructed with hazards at the back of the green as well. There is also nothing to stop you landing the ball a little short if you have a fairly straightforward chip and run to the pin.

With a straight-in approach and no trouble short of the green your safest shot on a long par-3 could be to land it on the front of the green, again taking

all the risk out of your shot, though you must always take into account the wind. Again, far too often I see players in pro-ams just picking up a 5-iron if the distance is 160 yards, irrespective of whether the shot is uphill or downhill, into the wind or with it.

On their local course they also tend to take just one club, week in, week out, summer or winter, for each par-3. Yet the shot can vary between a 7-iron one day, with a strong tail-wind, and a driver the next, into a howling gale. The golf course changes its character every day so play the golf course as it is when you play it now, not how it was yesterday.

Another problem on par-3s is that many golfers are embarrassed to take out a wood, feeling it is the proper thing to do to hit an iron.

There is nothing wrong with hitting a wood on a par-3. Indeed, a little 5-wood could be the best club possible on a par-3 of between about 180–220 yards, and there are plenty of par-3s of that length these days. It is a great club because it has a lot of loft and will get the ball nice and high, as well as a good distance, before bringing it down softly on the green.

If the hole is even longer you could use anything up to a driver, for at the end of the round, when you hand your card in, they don't ask you what clubs you used on each hole; they ask what your score was.

I always tee the ball on a par-3, having it very low, but I like to give it the very best lie I can. Elsewhere on the course you do not have this advantage, so whenever I have the opportunity, I take it. You should do the same.

The photographs on these two pages and the next two will show you how I set up to play a par-3 hole. This one is fairly long, being 190 yards with a carry across water to a green guarded by bunkers left and at the back.

I have teed the ball because I think it is important to get as perfect a lie as possible. When you have the chance I think you should take it.

I have the ball a little further back in my stance, just forward of centre, and have a slow, low takeaway. From the top of the backswing, where, again, my shoulders have really turned well, with my left shoulder under my chin, the hands pull down hard as my weight begins transferring to the left.

Once again my body completes the swing by turning to the left, facing the target at the finish.

The par-3 tee shot from another angle. See how I bring the club back without breaking my wrists at this stage. You must keep your left arm fairly straight.

Opposite page: *With the ball inside my left heel I take the club away smoothly, keeping my left arm straight. A full shoulder turn gets the swing arc wide, then allowing me to transfer my weight to the left as my hands pull down hard on the club.*

It is important to keep your head fairly steady over the ball as you swing the club to the top of the backswing before pulling down hard.

The weight is transferring as I pull the club-head down into impact, then following through as my body turns to face the target.

LONG IRONS AND FAIRWAY WOODS

People seem to get very scared over using long irons and, as I said a little earlier when we were looking at the distances we hit the golf ball, many golfers do not get full value from the longer irons in terms of distance.

The face of a long iron is straighter than the short irons and the fact that the ball is sitting down on the ground and not teed up causes a lot of golfers concern. What they need to do is to hit the shot with a smooth, very long controlled swing, never a punch.

With a short iron you come down crisply into the back of the ball, punching it away. With a long iron you do not pick the club up in the air, nor must you chop down with it. It's a long, full swing that is very important.

With the long irons you need to extend the clubhead through impact and carry on, the club still moving outside a little more, just as you do with a fairway wood. You will get a long shot from these irons if you remember that it is a long, flowing swing.

You need to look carefully at the shot you have in front of you and remember that the only difference between a 2-iron and a 7-iron is in the length of the shaft, and the loft of the clubface.

The 2-iron will hit the ball further but lower, so it's no good suddenly taking the 2-iron from the bag and thinking you have to hit it completely differently, or of being frightened of it.

Too many golfers can only hit their

2-iron 240 yards once; at other times they get little more distance than from the 5-iron, yet if they forget that it's a different club and just swing through it, as they would for a 5-wood, the ball will get the proper distance every time.

It is always best, if possible with the shot you have in front of you, to hit the long irons with a little draw, unlike the short irons which are best hit with a little fade, something we shall come on to in a little while.

Take the club back on the inside with a very full backswing and shoulder turn,

Try to hit your long irons with a little draw, standing slightly closed at address.

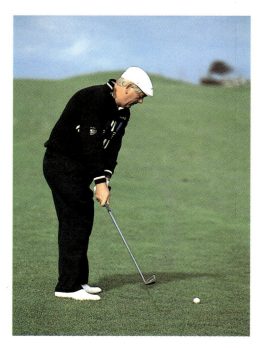

the weight really getting onto the right heel for right handed players, onto the left heel for left handers. This is now the area of golf where you need the legs to start driving down and forward, keeping the club going low through the ball and getting a full follow through. That is producing the power on these long shots.

Long iron play is, then, a matter of

Take the club back a little more on the inside as that will help you to produce a draw, getting a full shoulder turn, your left shoulder being under your chin at the top of the back-swing. Then pull down hard with your hands as you begin to transfer your weight left.

getting a full shoulder turn on the back-swing and a full follow through with the weight finishing on the left side, for right handed golfers; on the right side for left handed golfers.

On sloping lies, which we shall be dealing with a little later, the same principles apply, though if you are on a severe slope be careful in using the longer clubs as you may find your best option is to lay up to a safe spot.

After impact you must keep hitting through the shot, the clubhead continuing slightly outside as the hands release and the body turns to the left to a high, balanced finish.

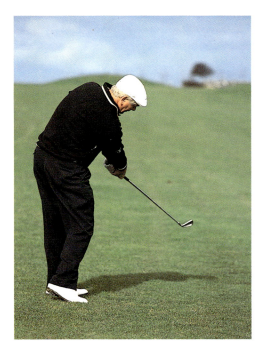

FAIRWAY WOODS

3-wood

I love using fairway woods and always look forward to creaming these off the fairway, but a lot of people, as with the driver, slice them because they try to get underneath the ball.

Earlier I showed you how to swing the driver through properly using two tee-pegs in the ground, trying to hit both as you swing the club through low and long. Use the same exercise here if you want to improve your fairway wood shots but this time push the tee-pegs further into the ground, about one inch

Stand very slightly closed for this shot, the ball inside the left heel. The shot I have here is 240 yards uphill.

showing. The idea here, too, is to get both these tee-pegs out of the ground as you swing through and I suggest you set them with the front one slightly outside the line, forcing you to swing with more of a draw shot, which again is the ideal shape for this shot.

You must get the club moving in that in-to-out swing pattern through impact to get the best from the fairway woods, though it is possible to shape them the other way, too, when you need to.

Again for this shot you should stand slightly closed at address, the right shoulder tucked neatly inside the left, but not too much.

As you take the club away it should come smoothly back just inside the line; again not too much but just enough to be able to attack the ball from just inside.

You need a good shoulder turn on the backswing, with your weight moving to the right heel, then sweep through the ball, making the club stay low as long as possible, unlike the iron shots. This is where the exercise with the two tee-pegs comes in handy.

The follow through is also vital here and you should keep in mind that the shot is never hit until the follow through is complete. It's no good just hitting at the ball and stopping. You must continue through into a good finish with your weight transferring totally to your left side.

You need a lot of leg action on this shot with your right knee driving through impact and onto the left side.

A lot of problems with this club come from a reverse pivot on the backswing. The weight must transfer both ways – to the right on the backswing, though not swaying – and onto the left side through impact.

I always think of a child's swing. The rope or chain holding the swing never slackens whilst the child is swinging – it always remains taut. That is because the weight of the child on the swing is transferring fully each time he or she swings. Your swing must have the same width and weight transfer to it all the time. With a full turn you will never get a reverse pivot and will be swinging with your entire weight rather than just with your arms.

The 3-wood is an excellent club to have in the bag because of its loft and distance. Apart from its use from the fairway it can be very good to use on a tight driving hole where you need to make sure you are accurate, possibly sacrificing a few yards but being certain that you hit the middle of the fairway.

I also like to use it from the tee of some holes if there is a hazard that I want to avoid, laying the ball up short.

The arms continue swinging the club back inside and up, with the left arm being kept comfortably straight.

Take the club away smoothly inside the line, keeping it low to begin with.

At the top of the backswing (above) the shoulders have fully turned, giving width to the swing arc. The downswing begins (left) with the hands pulling down hard on the club, as though you are pulling a bell rope. Near impact (below) the hands are squaring the clubface and the right knee beginning to kick round to the left, transferring the weight to the left side.

Just after impact (above), with the ball well on its way, I continue turning to the left as the arms continue swinging the club through impact. The body continues turning (right) to push on into a full, high finish (below). Remember, you have never hit the shot until you have reached the top of the follow through.

5-wood

The 5-wood is the 'working club' in the bag and one that I would be loathe to leave out. Just like my uncle before me I have learnt to love this club as it has so many uses. A lot of professionals leave one club out of the bag to make room for a third wedge. The 5-wood is one club I would never leave out. The one I use is a Tommy Armour Escapader and it is ideal, especially in rough grass.

This is one time you hit the ball the other way, from left to right in the air. If the ball is sitting down in the rough set the ball just inside the left heel with a very slightly tighter grip on the club with the left hand. Take the club away with just a hint of a high takeaway but do be careful not to break the wrists too

The 5-wood is ideal out of rough grass and you should adopt a slightly narrower but square stance.

much. Get into a good, high backswing, the shoulders turning well.

You then pull the club down hard from the top, the hands pulling down firmly. At the same time you need good leg action through this shot – never fall back on the right heel.

With a poor lie, even with only about 160 yards or so to the green, the 5-wood is a far better bet than the 5- or 6-irons, which would have trouble cutting through the long grass.

The 5-wood will cut through it perfectly and get enough elevation on the ball to get it safely to the green.

Grip down on it more, adopt a very slightly narrower but square stance, swing it up nicely and hit down and slightly across the ball. That will get you all the elevation you need without hitting the ball too far.

This club is well worth working hard with, because it really is so versatile and can be used for anything between about 150 and 240 yards. Any time you are in trouble grip down on the club for better control and hit it smoothly with a good rhythm and weight transfer. Again, that weight transfer is very important and you must avoid just flicking at the ball with your arms.

Use your body to generate power by making sure you build a good, wide backswing and then drive through the shot with your right knee kicking left and transferring your weight.

The takeaway is slightly steeper than with a 3-wood, but don't pick it up. Get a good shoulder turn and then pull down with the hands.

Continue swinging down and through, getting the weight transfer correct as you come through impact and driving the shot.

THE SCORING CLUBS

Whilst, with long irons, you should be looking to hit the ball quite a reasonable distance, getting green-high if not pin-high, with the shorter irons, from the 5-iron to the wedge, you should be looking to get the ball close to the hole.

The long irons are made for distance rather than the pinpoint accuracy you might like. The professionals in Tour events earn their living from hitting long irons to a position close to the pin, but if you miss the green short, or to the left or right, don't get too unhappy.

I always think club golfers have done well to get the ball near the green with the long irons, setting up a possible par if they have honed their short game skills.

With the 5-iron to the wedge, though, you should be hitting the green on a regular basis to set up a safe par or even, now and again getting the ball that close to the pin that you can give yourself a little birdie – something that will make your day.

Once again, though, you will never be able to do that unless you can learn to shape your shots with these clubs, hitting some high, some low, some with fade and some with draw.

Shot-making is a skill but it is so easy to make the small adjustments that are necessary to allow you to shape the ball at will. The place to learn these shots is on the practice range, not on the course. If you have learnt how to shape

them on the practice ground you will have the confidence to produce them on the course whenever you need to.

The Draw

Let's look, first, at drawing a 5-iron. There are three reasons you might want to do this. First, if you are faced with a slight dog-leg left and need to move the ball round to the left. Secondly, you might have some bunkers or other

A draw is the best shape of shot and you can play it with any club. Set up a little more closed than normal.

hazards guarding the left approach to the green and wish to work the ball away from them but still come in more from the right.

Thirdly, you might be playing the shot in a stiff breeze coming over your left shoulder at address – a left-to-right wind. For left handed golfers these directions need to be reversed, with a need to move the ball left to right.

One major problem club golfers have, in wind, is trying to pull the ball into the wind to hold it up. That is very bad. What you really need to do is to *spin* the ball into the wind.

Turn fully on the backswing as always.

The takeaway comes well inside the line.

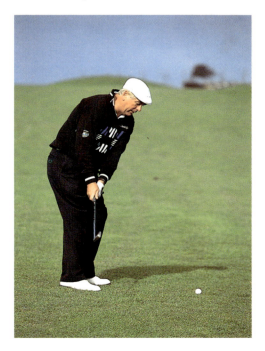

The way to do this is to aim a little right of your target, so that your right shoulder is tucked quite firmly inside the left at address. If you want to improve this shot even more show one more knuckle on the left hand, holding it very slightly stronger, though don't move the right hand grip.

Take a normal swing, getting your shoulders turned fully on the back-swing. Then, as you hit through the ball, your hands are moving slightly in-to-out. You must let them release properly but as they do this they are still moving very slightly outside, going through the shot the way the ball will be shaped.

If you pull them inside too quickly you will lose the shape of this shot by helping the wind to turn the ball over. A fade will result.

I mentioned earlier about extending the clubhead through the ball outside the line. The hands have to hold this on this shot.

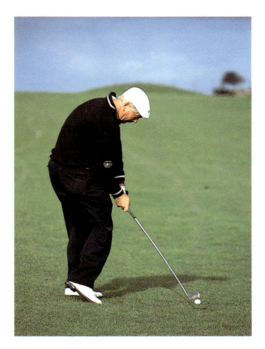

As you swing through you must have the feeling that you are going to push the hands outside before they release and come back inside for a high finish (below). On the right is the real impact position and follow through, but note how the club is attacking the ball from inside to shape this shot.

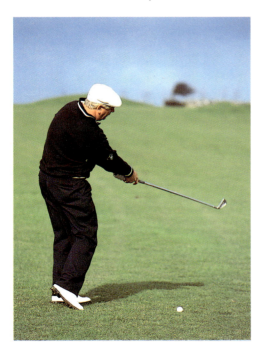

The Fade

Now for a fade with the scoring clubs, and although I am using a 5-iron to show you how to play these shots you can play them with any of the clubs, though you will get better results in shaping shots with the straighter faced clubs.

You might want to fade the ball into the green if you are playing in a right-to-left wind or if there is a potential hazard on the right approach of the green. A ball hitting the green with fade spin will stop faster than one hitting the green with draw spin, and once you have learnt to play these shots you will find that you can use them to your advantage so many times.

To fade the ball, aim left of the green, your shoulders a little open but don't overdo it. I would rather see you stand square and then just turn slightly to your left, aiming everything that way. The club will now move back slightly outside the target line and come across the ball, spinning it to the right, fighting the right-to-left wind.

One very important point to take into account on all these shots is to make sure you take enough club.

From the beginning of this book you will remember that I told you to keep a note of your distances with each club. In the wind – even a side wind – allow one more club to compensate for the wind. In strong wind you may need to

take two clubs more and it's much easier to take the extra club and swing within yourself rather than trying to knock the stuffing out of the ball. If you do slightly overhit and land the ball on the back of the green, so what?

It's better to be there than to be in the bunker short of the green.

You have made a note of your yardages – stick to them. Always swing the club smoothly, rather than straining to hit it at 101% of your capacity.

If you want more distance, hit more club – that's what you paid for!

To fade the ball set up slightly open to the target.

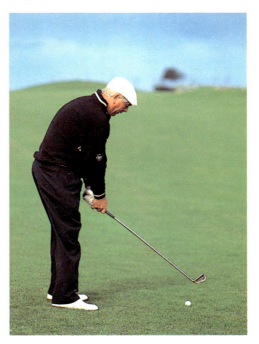

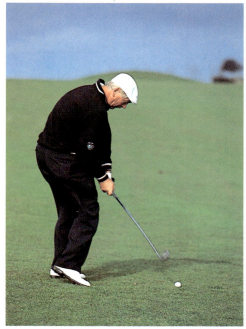

You can see (above) that the club does not move quite so far inside on the takeaway. You are still getting a good shoulder turn (above right) with the club swinging more along the body line rather than the ball to target line. This shows quite well (right) as I approach the impact zone. Don't hold back on this shot.

Just after impact (above left) the hands are being pulled inside and the weight continues through, getting distance and shape on the ball as it starts left of its target before turning in mid air (left). Get to a good finish, facing a little left of the target here (above).

Low Shots

Low shots are very important in wind, and playing on the wonderful links courses of Ireland and Scotland you are never far away from wind, I can assure you. Hitting the ball low into the wind is one of the finest shots you can use on a links course.

The main thing about this shot is to keep it smooth. Because you may be hitting the ball into the wind the temptation is always there to try to hit harder.

That does not work because all that does is put extra spin on the ball, just making it climb higher. That is giving the wind even more opportunity to knock it down. Never quicken your swing on a shot into the wind.

Set the ball closer to the right toe at address, midway between the centre and back of your stance, so that the club is hooded a little, with your hands slightly in front of the ball, just as you would for a short pitch to the green.

Once again, as I have said so often before, grip down the club for more control. Getting that extra control is so easy.

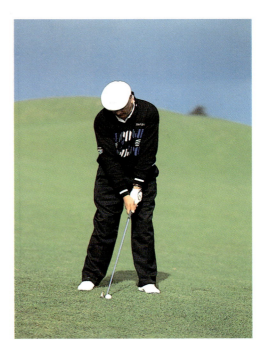

To hit the ball low address it further back; I have it just inside my right heel. Note how I have gripped down on the club for extra control. Make a full turn with the left shoulder getting under the chin, even though the swing is only three-quarters.

I think your stance should be slightly narrower for this shot, but you still need a good shoulder turn and weight transfer back and through the ball, getting your shoulders fully turned on the backswing. You can check by seeing that your left shoulder gets right under your chin on the backswing. For left handed golfers, the right shoulder must be under the chin at the top of the backswing.

Although you turn your shoulders fully you will only need to swing your arms up to about three-quarters for this shot. You need very firm wrist action on this shot but by that I do not mean that you flick your wrists at it.

You hit from the top but your wrists stay firm through the shot. Remember our thought of pulling the bell rope down from earlier.

You must pull down hard and then continue through with a full weight transfer, the legs driving down and left through impact, so that you finish with your weight on your left side and your

At impact your hands do not release but continue driving the clubhead through the shot.

Finish with both hands held out in front of you, though they may be slightly left of the target.

hands held out in front of your face, pointing at the target.

On this occasion your arms do not continue through to that full finish, but your weight must fully transfer. That is most important.

After impact, as your arms swing up your hands might have moved slightly to the left of the target but that is not a major problem. The main idea is to finish with both arms held rigid out in front of you rather than letting the hands release. Don't let those wrists roll at impact.

This is a great shot to play and you should really practise it hard, particularly with something like a 7-iron. It will penetrate and stay low into the wind, getting the ball to where you want it in a controlled manner.

High Shots

Now for a high shot with the mid irons. These you might use when you need to hit over water or a large bunker, or when you want to stop the ball quickly on landing. You will also need this shot if you wish to play the ball over a tree, though do make sure you are far enough from the tree to get over with the club you are using.

I also use it when playing downwind and it is important that you learn this, rather than trying to bounce a ball in low as so many golfers do.

If you hit it high downwind the wind will still knock it down onto the green and if you do slightly overhit it you will only land on the back of the green, which is often softer and will be more receptive to the ball.

Play the ball a little further forward this time, just inside the left heel. Take a good backswing with the left arm held as straight as you can on the backswing. Pull down hard with your hands as the harder you pull down, the higher the ball will go.

You need good leg action on this shot, driving through the ball, though don't try to scoop it up in the air. Hit down.

As you come through impact your hands will release as normal and will finish high and to the left. That, too, will get the ball higher.

One little point about hitting downwind. The ball will normally go higher but will often be knocked down by the wind, particularly on tree-lined courses where the wind is strongest at the level of the tops of the trees, even if you cannot feel very much wind at ground level, so don't get tempted into taking less club than you need. Take the club for that distance.

This is a shot that will take a little practice to get right but once you have learnt it, and all the other shaped shots that we have dealt with here, you will find that it brings your scores down much faster than merely trying to knock the skin off the golf ball.

In this situation the ball needs to climb high out of some light rough so I have it further forward in my stance and take no more than a three-quarter backswing.

Opposite page: *Then pull down very hard with your hands. The harder you pull down the higher the ball will fly. Your legs must drive through this shot as it cannot be hit with just the arms. Follow through as always, but don't try to scoop the ball up. If you hit down, the ball will go up.*

RECOVERY SHOTS

We all get into trouble from time to time – some more often than others! – but, when the ball has strayed from the straight and narrow you have one prime aim – get it back onto short grass, fast!

Sadly this is where so many club golfers go wrong. Many of them seem to forget that the ball is in trouble and take the club they normally would for a particular distance. If, for example, the ball is 150 yards from the green and in rough, many golfers take the 6-iron because that is what they need for a shot of 150 yards. They seem to forget, or ignore the fact that the ball is in the rough and will not, therefore, react as it would from the fairway.

It depends greatly on how thick the rough is and whether the ball is sitting up or is buried deep as to what you can do. If it is buried your only option might be to take a sand wedge and blast it out onto the fairway, but to a safe spot. If it is sitting up in fairly light rough you do have a good chance of hitting it cleanly to the green, but beware you don't get underneath it, leaving it short, or get a 'flier' from the grass – a ball that you will not be able to control once it lands on the green.

I shall deal with both of these situations, as well as those other troublesome shots around the green where the ball is in semi-rough. It's those type of shots that so many players make a mess of, because they fail to take the ball cleanly with enough loft and power on the clubface.

But let's look, first, at those shots from fairly thick rough the inhospitable parts of the golf course. I must say that I feel that some golf clubs let the rough grow too long, thus causing their members more problems than they should be faced with. A shot straying from the fairway should be punished, but you should be able to see the ball and be able to get a club at it, even if you can't hit a perfect shot.

When you are in an awkward situation your first thought must be to get the ball back on the short grass, fast!

With the ball sitting up with a half decent lie your prime aim is to get it back onto short grass. Your most lofted club might be the answer, providing you are not close to any overhanging branches which might catch it.

The club you use will depend on the distance you have to go but do bear in mind that, because grass will get between the clubface and the ball, you might get what we call a 'flier', the ball running on once it lands. It is, thus, easy to hit the ball too far and you might find that you hit out of rough on

With the ball sitting in rough grass use your most lofted clubs.

one side of the fairway only to see it roll into the trees on the other side!

In summer with a hard fairway that is even more likely so take your time to think about the shot before you play it. Whilst you don't need to spend all day playing one round of golf I do see far too many golfers in pro-ams playing their shots before they have properly thought about what it is they are trying to achieve.

I would suggest you tighten your left hand grip a little, as the grass will pull the club left as it hits into it, so the ball will always hook slightly.

You can compensate for this by aiming the club slightly right but be careful not to overdo it.

The shot is played with a crisp, chopping action, the club coming down steeply across the ball, missing most of the grass and getting to the ball as cleanly as possible.

The other thing you should do is to drag your right foot a little more rather than turning through impact as you do on a normal shot. You are, in effect, delaying the weight transfer and this will help get the ball out.

If the ball is sitting up well, do be careful that you do not slide the club too far under the ball as that will lose you some distance.

You can go some way to preventing this happening by keeping your full body weight moving through the ball, so that you are dragging the club

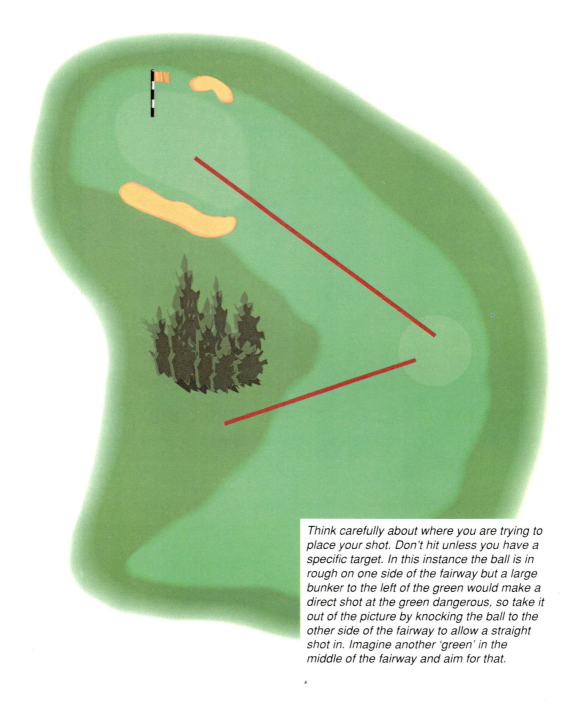

Think carefully about where you are trying to place your shot. Don't hit unless you have a specific target. In this instance the ball is in rough on one side of the fairway but a large bunker to the left of the green would make a direct shot at the green dangerous, so take it out of the picture by knocking the ball to the other side of the fairway to allow a straight shot in. Imagine another 'green' in the middle of the fairway and aim for that.

through the shot rather than trying to get underneath it, which would result in your falling back at impact.

With the ball deep in the rough where you can hardly see it, you need to pick the club up almost vertically on the backswing, so the club does not move inside as much as it does on a normal takeaway. That creates a steep descent into the ball as well, which is exactly what you want. You should have in your mind that you are aiming the heel of the club at the ball.

Gripping down the shaft will help you

Hit through the shot rather than getting under the ball.

to pick it up steeper, with a very early wrist-cock, as you do for a bunker shot. Although your follow-through will be cut off by the thick grass you need to build into your swing the idea that you are going to have a full follow-through.

By this I mean that you should always plan your swing as though you were going to follow through to a full, high finish, just as you would from the fairway. Your mind should have decided that the hands and arms were going to swing the club the whole way through, with no intention of stopping. Although the thick grass will restrict your follow-through you must have the intention of cutting through the grass and making that full follow-through. Never quit as you hit the ball.

When you are playing from the rough make sure that you do know where you are going. Choose your spot carefully, one that will make your next shot a clear one to the green – or other target on a long par-5. If there are bunkers on one side of the green try to get into a position where you do not have to play towards them. You need to have in mind an imaginary green in the middle of the fairway, in a spot that will give you an ideal next shot, and aim your shot out of the rough to this imaginary green. Try it and you will find it focuses your attention much better than just trying to hit the ball out. Always have a specific target in mind.

Rough round the green causes a great

Aim for the fat of the green rather than taking risks by playing straight at the pin.

Your sand wedge is the best club to use when you need a very lofted shot to get the ball up and over a hazard very quickly, but if you have a lot of green to work with a less lofted club will do fine. You will find that all professionals carry at least one extra wedge, preferring to have more choice in these 'scoring' clubs, and leaving out one of the woods or long irons.

Remember you can only have a maximum of fourteen, including the putter. Go to your local professional and ask to try a few wedges and sand wedges until you find one you are really comfortable with. It may even be the one you already have.

For deep rough around the green, stand open with your feet very close together and aim to hit across the ball about an inch behind it, very much like a bunker shot. You will again find it helps to grip down on the club for more control and to assist you with a steeper takeaway, the club coming up almost vertically and outside the target line.

A major problem in this shot is the risk of thinning it, which will send it flying across the green and into more trouble on the other side. To avoid this get very low to the ball, even bending your knees a little more but, more than anything, trying to hit an imaginary ball deeper in the ground than the real one. This will force you to slide the club really low under the ball, the loft on the clubface just lifting it out

deal of problems for most golfers yet if you play the shot properly you will be surprised at your success rate. Normally, a ball coming out of rough and landing on the green will run some distance so be very aware of how far you need to hit the ball. For that reason I suggest you normally aim for the fat of the green, particularly if the pin is cut very close to your side of the green, or if it is cut in a position that leaves you very little room for error. Although a short uphill putt is the ideal, never be afraid of going past the pin.

smoothly. I have seen some golfers trying to stand rigid on this shot but it does require some leg action to generate enough power to get the ball safely out, so don't try to just use your arms and shoulders and keep your legs and feet totally still. Swing gently through the shot, moving your weight just enough to get the ball out.

The best place to practise this shot is out of rough going uphill to a practice green because you then have to generate enough power to get the ball out and up the slope. Stand about ten yards back from the edge of the green and the steeper the slope the better it is for this practice routine.

Never stab at this shot, nor try to scoop it. The hand action needs very carefully looking at too, for the left hand should be in front of the ball for as long as possible, pulling the club low under the ball.

Your follow through is very short but do go through the shot completely.

Ladies are often much better players around the green because, lacking the extra power that men have, they have to play a fuller shot, but gently.

You may sometimes be on the fringe of the green itself, the ball up against the longer grass where it would be very difficult to get a putter at it.

The ideal thing to do here is to 'belly' a sand wedge at the ball, the leading edge of the club just catching the equator of the ball, sending it out low

with enough roll to reach the hole.

Address the ball on its equator with the blade pointing directly at your target. Again grip down on the shaft for more control and then gently swing back and across the ball, the flange of the club almost catching the ball and knocking it forward.

It will stay very low, just like a putt and you should treat it that way, extending the club directly at the target as you would for a long putt.

You will normally have some distance

With the ball against a fringe of longer grass I would normally hit it with the leading edge of the sand wedge, 'blading' the ball.

to go with this shot so don't leave it short. Make sure you do hit it hard enough to get through the rough grass.

Once again, adopt a very narrow stance, your feet almost together and address the ball more off your right toe than the middle of your stance. Again that keeps the left hand ahead of the ball as long as possible.

Moving back a little you do sometimes have the chance to putt from off the green though you must only do so if there are no problems in the way, no severe slopes, no long grass and you are no more than about three yards off the front edge of the green. Any more than that and you should play a different club. This is a shot you must practise to get your distances right but remember, you do not need power around the green – you need touch.

Hit the ball on the equator so that you send it running with topspin and always take the putter back inside the target line so that you are hitting the ball from the inside, just as you would if you were deliberately trying to hook the ball. This will keep it going longer and straighter.

If you are a little further back, or you consider the putter is not the best club to use you can choose a 6- or 7-iron.

The ball will stay very low, but make sure you do follow through with the clubhead, rather as you would with a long putt.

You can putt from off the green but I would never go too far back or you might give yourself problems.

Left: *Address the ball with the putter head level with the equator of the ball. This will make the ball run straighter and longer.*

Play it exactly as you would for a putt, standing well open, use your putting grip and keep your wrists stiff through the shot, as you do on the green with the putter, with your hands well ahead of the ball and your eye firmly on it. See the photographs right and on the opposite page.

The area around the green is not always flat, of course, so you will sometimes have either an uphill chip or the slightly more difficult downhill chip. I'll begin with the uphill.

This shot often fools a lot of golfers because they, once again, do not fully understand how the golf club works. Most golfers try to hit the ball up when they should be hitting it forward towards the bank in front of them. The clubface gets the ball up. It may sound like splitting hairs but you really need to understand this. You only ever hit the ball forwards (there are one or two tiny exceptions when you are in the face of a very steep bunker or bank), the clubface is built with enough loft to get the ball in the air. Concentrate on hitting forward and leave the club to do the rest.

To hit uphill to the green (this is a fairly short shot we are discussing) have the ball positioned off the right toe, the clubface a little right of your target, your hands well in front of the ball at address and drive the club down into the ball.

I like to have my hands just about opposite my right knee. That squeezes it forwards which is all you should be

Set up with the ball well back, your hands ahead of the ball and concentrate on hitting the ball forward. The loft on the clubface will get it airborne.

thinking of. Leave the clubface to do its work of getting the ball up in the air. Put out of your mind any thoughts of trying to hit it up – just hit it forwards.

You can be quite aggressive with this shot because it will stop quickly on landing so you can afford to go for the pin, unless it is cut in such a difficult position that there is little room for error, in which case aim for the fat of the green.

Downhill shots around the green can be more difficult, but most people again concentrate on getting the ball up rather than getting it forwards, and so often leave the ball short.

On this shot you need to stand more open, so that you can cut across the ball, but with a firm action rather than a wristy flick at the ball, which is the fault of many higher handicap players.

Always look to land the ball on the flat putting surface, even if the pin is cut very close to your side of the green. It is always better to be putting from past the flag, even if that is downhill, than to have the ball short in the bunker or rough.

Restrict your backswing to no more than about two feet and go through the ball the same amount, though don't

If you want the ball to run on landing you must release your hands, the right rotating over the left through impact. If you don't release them the ball will stop quickly.

deliberately try to cut it off or you risk quitting on the shot and leaving it short. You do, though, keep the hands working together and firm, so that you finish with the back of your left hand, and the clubface itself, at the target.

Left handed players need to reverse this so that they play the ball off the left toe with their right hand above the left knee, and keep the back of the right hand at the target through the shot rather than releasing the hands so that the left hand rolls over the right.

This non-release of the hands is important for all the short shots that we have covered so far but as I said, if you want the ball to continue rolling you should release your hands at impact.

Right: *On short shots if you want the ball to stop quickly, hold the follow through, the back of your left hand ending pointing at the target. If you want the ball to run, release the hands through impact.*
Below: *With a downhill chip stand open and swing steeply into the ball.*

It is always amazing how a lake or other water hazard running down the side of a fairway, or crossing the approach to a green has a magnetic effect on golf balls! Players who, week in, week out, quite easily hit the ball fairly straight, or carry the ball to the safety of the green on an approach, go to pieces once there is water on the course – and I don't mean rain!

There is a huge psychological problem here for many golfers and although it is easy for me to tell you to forget the water, the fact is, it's there.

One thing about water is that it is nearly always a longer carry than it looks, because water is flat and reflects the sky, so is lighter than the fairway. Distances tend to become slightly distorted because of this so I suggest you look carefully at any yardage charts you have available and take careful note of them, rather than merely trusting your eyes.

If in doubt, or if you have no charts to help you, tend to the longer side, particularly if you are hitting an approach to a green. There is nothing wrong with aiming for the back of the

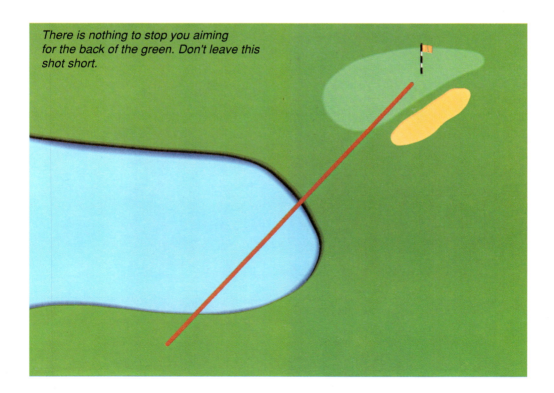

There is nothing to stop you aiming for the back of the green. Don't leave this shot short.

green, which is often softer and thus more receptive than the front of the green – primarily because less people go there.

When hitting over water take extra club, grip down a little and play the ball very slightly further back in your stance. That will help you hit down into the back of the ball, cutting out any risk of a thinned shot and easily carrying the water. Don't try to scoop the ball up and don't try to hit it extra distance – just let the golf club do the

Swing with your normal rhythm – ignore the water.

When hitting over water always make sure you have enough club, even if it means taking a 5-wood.

work it was designed for, something I have said before and will continue to say. If you need more distance take more club. Don't swing faster or try to hit harder, use the rhythm you have built up.

When there is no water and you have a fairly flat approach to the green, with no hazards directly on your line, I suggest you use something like a 7-iron, though if you are further away you could use an 8- or 9-iron.

Try each club in similar circumstances so that you can understand how each club will hit the ball. The longer irons will normally hit the ball further but on a lower trajectory so you will soon discover how much time the ball spends in the air and how much rolling. You must always get the ball airborne, though, even if only a couple of feet.

To play this shot stand with a fairly open stance, your feet quite close together, which forces you to use your hands and arms more, rather than just relying on the body turn to generate the power.

This shot needs 'feel' rather than force. Play the ball well back in your stance, almost off your right toe. As you take the club away from the ball keep it low and slow, visualising where you want the ball to land. Always remember that if you are hitting slightly downhill the ball will roll more on landing.

A very good practice routine to help you perfect this shot is to try to pitch balls into an upturned umbrella about twenty yards away. As your aim on the golf course is to get the ball within a six-feet circle of the hole you will find this exercise a great help.

The hands control this shot and if you have only a short distance to go you do not release your hands, keeping the back of your left hand and the clubface

If you are hitting across a dip to the green you have two shots. Either pitch at the pin itself, if there is sufficient green to work with; or, with the pin close, chip the ball to the edge of the upslope and it will gently roll.

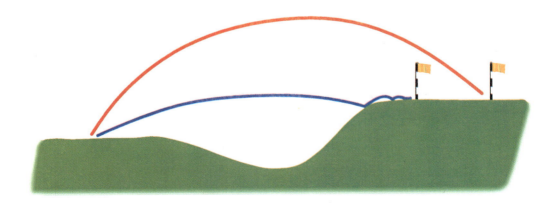

pointing towards the target in the follow-through. If, however, you want the ball to run extra distance once it hits the green, let the hands release as you come through the ball, so that they finish with the fingers of the right hand pointing at the target and the clubface parallel to the target line.

There are occasions when you are hitting to a green that is on the same level as you are, but with a dip in the ground between you and the front of the green. You have two different shots to play here, depending on the distance between the front of the green and the pin. If the pin is some way on the green your best choice is to pitch directly at the pin, letting the ball carry the dip and land on the flat surface.

If, however, the pin is cut very close to the edge of the green and you are worried about going too far past, particularly on hard, fast greens in summer, pitch the ball to land close to the top of the upslope where, once it lands, the grass and slope will deaden it, letting it just roll onto the green gently. To play this second shot hood the club with your hands well ahead of the ball, adopt a fairly narrow stance, your feet maybe about eight inches apart and slightly open to the target.

If the approach is flatter, with just a hint of a depression between you and the green there is nothing wrong with playing a putt with something like a 6-iron. Play this exactly as you would

with your putter. It is an easy shot that many golfers fail to use yet it is very effective in the right circumstances.

Again I must suggest you go out to the practice range and try all these shots, playing off varying lengths of grass rather than finding a perfect lie every time.

Only by doing this will you learn both the capabilities of your set of golf clubs, and your own. Always choose a definite landing area and check that it is safe for the type of shot you are playing.

Always have a definite target in mind – the place you want the ball to land, not finish.

When hitting a shot over water to a tight pin position, aim for the fat of the green and hit down hard into the back of the ball, gripping down more on the club for extra control. Make sure you have enough club for the distance, plus a little extra, and follow through fully.

BUNKERS

Most club golfers hate bunkers. Ironically, perhaps because they hate them so much, very few golfers practise in bunkers enough or, more importantly, take a lesson from their golf professional on bunker play.

Rather than going to the driving range and trying to knock the skin off a few dozen golf balls, go to your club professional and have half an hour with him learning how to play bunker shots. You will save more shots that way, I guarantee.

To get the ball out of a bunker you need to get the ball up in the air. For this reason I would urge you never to use a putter out of bunkers, although I have seen people try.

Sand is very unpredictable in its consistency and you can never be certain that the ball will come out as you want it. You are always better playing a sand wedge a short distance.

I'll begin with greenside bunkers which are by far the most common. Unlike shots from the fairway, with a bunker shot you don't want to hit the ball but to bounce the club under it. To understand this fully I want you to imagine that the ball is sitting nicely on the surface of the sand but that, buried under the ball, maybe two or three inches down, is a piece of wood about ten inches long.

The ideal shot would be one where the clubhead enters the sand two inches behind the ball, hits down onto this piece of wood, then comes up out of the sand as you swing through.

Next time you are in a bunker imagine that, under the ball is that piece of wood. Your aim is not to hit the ball but to hit the piece of wood.

Try to imagine a piece of wood is under the ball and you have to hit it before bringing the club back up.

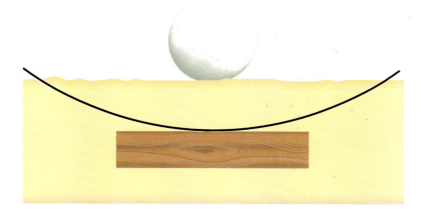

That thought should make you hit down and under the ball rather than trying to hit the ball itself. You also have to get the clubhead the whole way through to a good finish rather than leaving it in the sand, again something too many higher handicap players do. You must never quit on this shot.

For a fairly short bunker shot from a greenside bunker stand with your feet about six inches open, the ball in about the middle of your stance.

The club is picked up very steeply, with a very early wrist-cock – the wrists almost cocking before the arms begin pulling the club back.

The backswing is very steep, almost vertical away from the ball, and the swing takes the club well outside the line. This makes you bring the club down very sharply across the ball,

You must get the clubhead under the sand. This is how far down I go.

The sand wedge has a wide, low flange which helps it bounce through sand rather than digging in.

remembering to skim the club into the sand a couple of inches behind the ball, to hit that imaginary piece of wood a couple of inches down and, vitally, to follow through to quite a high finish.

The length of the backswing varies but do make sure it is long enough to generate the power needed to get the

Opposite page: *From an open stance (top left), swing the club back fairly steeply along the body line, not the target line. Pull down hard and continue to hit through impact, getting to a full finish.*

clubhead through the sand without slowing down. You should swing the club up to at least shoulder height on the backswing; the follow-through the same length or longer, if possible.

One way to vary the length of the shot is by standing more or less open. The shorter the shot you want to hit the more open you stand. That's easy to remember.

The closer you are to the pin the more open you stand.

Plugged

If the ball is plugged you have a slightly more difficult shot, primarily because you will be unable to control the ball once it stops.

Stand a little more square to the ball and hood the clubface more. Have the feeling that, as you reach the top of the backswing you are aiming the end of the shaft (the grip end) directly down at the ball. Because you stand a little more square to this shot you are not taking the club so far outside the line on the backswing but there is still a fairly steep takeaway from the ball, bringing the club down across the ball slightly and lifting it out though with not as much height as previously.

If the bunker has a very high lip you should think carefully about your options as the ball will not rise too much. It will, as I said, also run thirty to forty feet on landing so you need to have enough green to work with. The one thing you must avoid is hitting it out of one bunker only to see it run into a bunker on the other side of the green. Play sensibly and, if there is any doubt in your mind about the shot, play to the fat of the green or even off the green itself to a position where you could have a safe and straightforward chip and run to the pin.

Don't take risks in bunkers as your one aim is to get the ball out first time.

Playing from a plugged lie in sand. Stand rather more square and take the club away fairly steeply on your body line. The club will then come down sharply across the ball and lift it out, though as you will see on the next page it will stay lower and run more once it lands, so you need to aim at an area of green where you have sufficient room.

Long Bunker Shots

By this I mean a shot from a greenside bunker that is fairly long. Normally you will be in the back edge of the bunker with a lot of sand to cover before you reach the green. The pin may then be fairly close to your side of the green.

These are far more difficult shots and you will do well to land the ball safely on the green.

Look very carefully at alternative options. If you can get the ball out of the sand to a safe chip and run distance I would suggest you think very carefully about that.

To play the shot, though, have the ball well forward in your stance with the clubface as open as you can get it, so that, at address, the blade is pointing to the sky.

This is a full swing with the sand wedge. The club is taken away well outside the line and fairly steeply, but you need to really drive the club through and under the ball, hitting downwards as you come across and under the ball.

The shot is played with a full hand release coming through the ball – don't

As the ball comes out from this lie it will run so do make sure you have enough green to work with.

try to cut this off, but play it just as a normal shot.

You have to hit the ball, or rather the sand just under it, very hard. Choose your target very carefully as the ball will again run on landing rather than pulling up quickly, so you need to have plenty of green to work with.

With a longer bunker shot you do not stand quite so open. Have the ball further forward in your stance. Take a fairly full backswing and release fully through the shot.

Longer Bunker Shots

You often come across bunkers about 50 yards or so from the green and, in many ways, these present you with a much easier shot. You need to hit the back of the ball as on a shot from the fairway, but I would suggest either the sand wedge or the wedge for this shot.

Even as you move much further back I would never recommend you take anything less than a 7-iron out of sand.

To hit the ball some distance take a full swing, take the ball cleanly but keep hitting through the shot, taking a divot of sand. Never try to lift or scoop the ball off totally cleanly with this bunker shot. You must drive the ball forward; the loft on the clubface gets it airborne.

It is very important to keep the left hand leading through this shot for right handed golfers. Left handed golfers must keep their right hand leading.

As with the previous shot on the last page, hit through this shot hard, your left hand leading throughout and your body turning through impact. Don't dig in behind the ball but don't be afraid to take a divot of sand.

Sloping Lies in Sand

Uphill shots in bunkers are fairly easy, even with the ball plugged. You need to remember that the ball will rise higher and travel less distance than from a flat lie so you often need to hit it harder to blast it out. You should think of hitting this with 150% power, drilling the club-face into the bunker face.

Although you may have a slight problem finding a decent place to stand, make sure you are well balanced before playing this shot as you must not lose your balance. Although you hit harder than normal don't take too long a backswing as that might pull you off-balance and the shot will be ruined.

Take a three-quarter backswing at most but then really drive the club into the bunker face, blasting the ball out high. The slope will cut off your follow through but you must have the swing thought in mind that you are going to drive straight through to a full finish. This means you use your knees and legs more than in normal bunker shots.

Shots from a downslope in bunkers are far more difficult. You need to stand very open, take a very full, slow swing way outside the line and come across

With this very awkward shot you stand very open, taking a steep backswing away from the ball to get as much height on the club as you can.

From the top of the backswing you must pull down hard, driving down and through the ball. Imagine you have another ball below the real ball.

the ball and go as deep as you can, again with the feeling that you are driving down through the sand. Aim into the sand about four inches behind the ball and don't let the club come up out of the sand too early.

You must keep driving it lower, as if you had a second ball buried six inches down that you needed to hit as well. You also need a lot of wrist action on this shot as you release your hands through impact very quickly. The ball will come out lower than for a normal shot sop once again will run on landing. Aim for the fat of the green or even away from the green to leave you a safe chip and run for the next shot.

Finally, before we leave the sand, a quick word about wet sand. Because the ball will come out firmer with less backspin you will have more trouble controlling it, so either allow for this in choosing your target or hit it less hard.

This does not mean that you swing the club limply at the ball, but swing slower, still getting through the ball at impact.

Your hands must release through the shot. Again with this shot the ball will come out very low so you must first ensure you hit it hard enough to get it safely across the bunker, but then you will need enough green to work with or you risk going through the green into possibly even more trouble.

SLOPING LIES

Fairways are not all flat and whilst many of the slopes you will encounter on the golf course will cause you no concern you may occasionally find one that is severe. Knowing how to play a shot from that slope is important if you are to become an accomplished golfer.

There are four main types of sloping situation you may encounter, apart from those in bunkers which I have dealt with already. You may have a shot from a downhill lie, one from an uphill lie, one with the ball below your feet and one with the ball above your feet.

Let's look, first, at the downhill lie where you have to hit the ball to a green below you. The ball will always fade or slice from this position, because of the way the club comes down into the ball, cutting slightly across it.

To compensate you need to aim slightly left, standing a little open to the target. Assuming your target is the green you should be aiming to the left edge of the green (right edge of the green for left handed players), going further or less left according to the severity of the slope. The steeper it is the more left you aim.

The ball should be positioned between the centre and back of your stance and I suggest you grip down on the club more than usual.

Your shoulders should be virtually level, not with the slope but as though you were standing on flat ground. Your

When you are hitting downhill you must set up aiming slightly left.

right shoulder is always a little lower than the left as you address the ball so don't try to stand in any position that makes you look like a contortionist. Your right knee, being further up the slope, will be flexed more to get you into the right position.

Take a three-quarter backswing and use good movement of the legs to drive through the ball, with your normal weight transfer. You must get the feeling that you are sweeping through this shot rather than hitting hard down into the back of it. Avoid hitting early and keep

The ball is positioned between the centre and back of your stance (left), allowing you to make a three-quarter backswing with your shoulders fairly level. As you stand on the slope your right knee is flexed more, or you would be standing at an odd angle (below left).

in mind the fact that the club needs to stay low after it has struck the ball. You should, once again, try to think about hitting a second ball a few inches beyond the real one.

Try it with a tee-peg placed in the ground about six inches in front of the ball. Your aim is to hit the ball, then the tee-peg.

Unlike a normal fade or sliced shot, which will fly high and stop quickly on landing, a shot from a downhill lie will not. This will fly lower and thus run more on landing so make sure you have the right club. If you have a hazard to carry in front of the green, such as a bunker or some water, you might need extra club, though do remember that the longer the club the lower the ball's trajectory.

I do see some players attempting to hit this shot and the photographs on the opposite page highlight them.

You can see that too long a backswing will pull you way out of position and you risk losing your balance. You must also avoid swaying the other way.

Trying to hit too hard will also pull you off balance. Maintain your rhythm.

Some common faults I see with playing from a downslope.

Above left: Too long a backswing will pull you out of position so only go back about three-quarters.

Above right: But don't sway backwards on the backswing.

Right: Swinging down too quickly into the ball will make you hit the ground long before you reach the ball.

With a ball below your feet you have to stretch more to get down to the ball and the swing becomes much steeper, as well as making the club cut across the ball more. You should, however, try to avoid taking the club outside the line on the backswing, trying to get it vertically back from the ball.

This shot will also fade, often quite severely, so aim well left (right for a left hander) to allow for this. Don't make the mistake of closing the clubface as that is not what you want. You must always alter your aim.

Your stance tends to be more over the ball and you will be gripping the end of the club to get as much length as you can. Don't overswing on this shot or you will lose your balance, but do, as with the previous shot, try to keep going down through the ball rather than swinging the club straight back up. Once again, imagine you have a further target a few inches in front of the ball and swing through to hit that. If you take your time these shots are easy.

With the ball below your feet you need to bend your knees (top left) and play the ball slightly back in your stance (left). Aim slightly left to compensate for the slope (opposite right, top), bending further to be near the ball. The backswing is fairly steep (below right) but only to three-quarters (top, far right). The clubhead is swung down and across the ball (bottom, far right) to another imaginary ball a few inches further on.

Uphill shots tend to create more problems for the average golfer, perhaps because they think they have to hit harder. As I have said elsewhere in this book you never hit harder to get the ball further – if you want to increase the distance take more club.

Going uphill the ball will draw, moving right to left in the air, because the swing makes the club come into the ball from in-to-out. The club is also hitting the ball on a slight upswing, the club having passed the nadir of its swing arc before it reaches the ball.

You should aim well right as the ball will have a lot of pull to the left of this lie. Because you are going uphill it will also fly higher than usual for the club you are using, so take care to choose the right club.

Once again set your shoulders fairly level, as if you had a spirit level across them and wanted to get the air bubble right in the centre.

Position the ball inside your left heel and grip down on the club for extra control, taking only a three-quarter backswing.

As you come into the ball use your right knee even more than usual, really pushing into the shot, driving your body up the slope rather than falling back as you hit the ball.

This is an exercise you can practise without a club. Stand as I have described and then swing your arms back as in the backswing; then, as you

Above: *Going uphill you stand a little closed.*

swing through to the impact position, push hard with your right leg to push you up the slope. That's the feeling you should get.

If you are hitting a ball up a slope and into the wind take care to take at least two clubs extra to compensate for the fact that, into the wind the ball will rise higher and travel less distance.

Opposite page: *You can see that I stand with the ball further forward in my stance and take a three-quarter swing. On the far right you can see that I emphasise the action of the right knee, which really must drive the weight up the slope to give power to this particular shot.*

Some swing faults when hitting uphill.

Above left: *This is a reverse pivot, leaning into the slope on the backswing.*

Above right: *The opposite, which will make you hit well behind the ball.*

Left: *Trying to make sure you hit the ball upwards will get you into this awful position. You will probably fail to hit the ball.*

With the ball above your feet you will also draw the ball left in the air (right for left handers), so you must aim to the right of the target.

As the ball is higher your swing is automatically flattened so stand closed to the target with the ball in the centre of your stance. Grip right down the club as far as you can, but even here your spine is likely to be almost upright, depending on the severity of the slope.

You will normally need extra club on

Aim a little right to compensate for the slope and swing back three-quarters once again, never overswinging. Get your right shoulder under the left to drive this shot at impact.

this shot because you are not able to get as much upper body movement through the swing. Take no more than a three-quarter backswing, swinging comfortably within yourself rather than losing your balance.

Again, as you hit through the ball try to keep your follow-through as low as possible, with that imaginary second ball or tee-peg a few inches in front of the ball.

On all shots from sloping lies do make extra sure that you get your right shoulder (left shoulder for left handed golfers) well under the left at impact. If you go the other way you will, in effect, be casting at the ball, throwing the club from the top of the backswing as you would cast a fishing line. The same really applies on all shots but is especially important on sloping lies.

Above left: *Too steep a backswing will make you cut across the ball.*

Left: *A similar fault with the club being swung back outside the line. That will really cut it away to the right.*

Opposite page top: *An uphill shot where you must really drive through with your right knee, powering the shot.*

Opposite page bottom: *With the ball below your feet stay balanced and only swing back three-quarters.*

PUTTING

P utting is often considered to be the most important part of the game of golf because it is the only time you score – when the ball finally drops in that little hole.

It is, then, pretty important and is often referred to as a game within a game, a phrase first coined by the great Bobby Jones.

I always try to set up square to the target, though many players stand a little open. Whatever the position of your feet you must make sure that your shoulders are square to the target as that is what dictates where the ball goes.

Keep your head very still on putting; you should hear the putt drop rather than see it on short putts and that is a very good practice routine, almost looking away to hear the ball drop in the cup.

I find it useful to walk round some putts to try to make sure the line I have seen when I walk onto the green is, in fact, correct. Take your time on putts.

Greens these days are, in most cases, very good so you can afford to go for the hole rather than trying to lag the ball up to within a few feet.

If you aim to go two feet past the hole every time you are giving yourself the very best chance of holing out.

I always aim for the back of the hole rather than trying to let it drop at the front. This may vary on some severely

Take your time on your putts, walking round the hole to check the borrow if necessary.

sloping greens like those at Augusta National, home of the US Masters where the greens undulate more than they appear on television.

The important point about putting is to keep very still and to keep your wrists out of the stroke, which must be controlled by the shoulders.

It's vital that you find your distances on the green and to do this I have a little practice routine that will help.

Put down some tee pegs, on the practice green at six feet, ten feet and

I putt with the ball just inside my left foot.

Catch the ball on the equator with the putter if you want it to roll true and straight.

Putting is something you must practise often. It accounts for half the game.

about twenty feet from where you are.

Putt two balls to each marker, repeating the process until you can get two extremely close to each one – and I mean almost touching.

Try it on sloping greens as well as flat ones, uphill as well as downhill. You must learn how the ball will turn on sloping greens, turning more as it slows down near the hole.

This is something you really have to do for yourself. All I can tell you is to keep those wrists out of the shot and to keep very still.

I putt with the putter face catching the ball on its equator, which helps to keep it rolling straight, the ball just inside my left foot.

Left and below: *Make sure that as you putt on very short putts, the putter is fully extended across the hole itself. That way you will be following through positively.*

Above and right: *Two putting faults. Don't let your wrists control this shot. On the backswing my wrists have cocked and therefore will flick at the ball going through. Avoid this.*

STRATEGY ON THE GOLF COURSE

Thinking your way round the golf course is probably 80% of the game, yet very few people give it this much thought. Most are more intent on knocking the stuffing out of the ball and trying to get the last inch out of every shot.

You do need to be positive, but be sensible. If you have a shot in hand over your opponent, use it, for at the end of a tournament you don't get double the prize money for winning by two shots rather than one.

The same thing applies for you if you are playing to your handicap and you receive an extra stroke on that hole. Of course you want to make a net birdie but only do so if you can do it sensibly, playing within yourself rather than trying to play at 101%.

You need to think your way round the golf course particularly towards the end of the round when, having been out there for two or maybe three hours, your concentration starts to lapse.

You also get to the stage where you begin trying different shots, maybe for a little bit of variety. Don't!

Carry on playing the way you have been playing all day. Keep your momentum going and concentrate on the shot you are playing, rather than thinking about making a birdie or having an extra shot on the 17th.

Don't let your mind play the next hole whilst your body is playing this

Take the time to think about your shot, 'seeing' it fully before you play it. You only have one chance to get it right.

one. In tournament play I never look around me; I don't look at the scoreboard to see who is in the lead. I try to avoid hearing what others are saying because I need to concentrate on the very next shot I have and only that one. The next hole will come along in its own time so only think of the one you are on now.

Always keep your head down and your heart up.

Never let other players' shots affect

you. That happened to Tony Jacklin a good few years ago at Muirfield when Lee Trevino hit a lucky shot to beat him in the Open. Everyone has their good breaks and their bad breaks.

Although it may seem that your opponent gets more good breaks than you on certain days he is probably just playing the course better, hitting less poor shots. Another day you will have more lucky breaks than him, so it evens itself up.

All you can keep doing is hitting good, solid shots within yourself and trying to beat par. Play the golf course, not your opponent. If you get beaten, you have not been beaten by your opponent but by the course. He may

Above: *A typical situation where you could go for the pin but that might be too dangerous, so play for the heart of the green on the left. That way you land on the putting surface and have two putts to save par.*

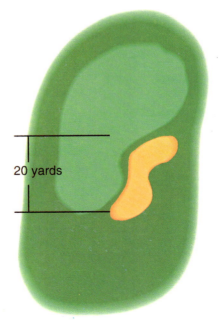

20 yards

Right: *The plan of this part of the hole.*

have played the course better than you but he has not beaten you. Only the course can beat you.

There are certain situations that you will encounter and although I cannot go through every conceivable golfing situation on the course, there are a couple of illustrations I would like to give you by way of an example. Understand these and you will be able to alter the circumstances to suit you.

The first is the situation where you have a shot to the green with the pin tucked tight behind a bunker on the right side of the green. This is the greenkeeper's art, placing the pin in a position that will be difficult for you to approach directly. That's his job.

Bunkers are often cut well into the green so there may be a 15 to 20 yard difference in length between the front of the green to the left, where it might be safe, and the front of the green over the bunker.

Take that into consideration in your calculations of which club to use, because you do not want to leave the ball either in the bunker or stuck on the bank with a more difficult shot.

I would almost always suggest you play to the heart of the green, but again do take the time to get your yardage correct. If you need to get close to the pin, if you are behind in a tournament and need to make up a stroke, for example, then by all means have a go but do be certain that you have the correct yardage and correct club.

Most yardage charts show the depth of the green and you can probably calculate the carry to clear the bunker. Add a good ten yards and then a little more for the pin location to that and hit fully with the correct club.

Another situation might be when you have to carry water off a downhill slope, with a chance to win the tournament.

If you are hitting from a downhill slope you are not going to get the ball as high as normal, though it may run

If you are hitting downhill across water the ball will fly lower, so make sure you have enough club.

longer. That could well mean that you will land it in the water or even on the upslope before the green. Neither is going to help you. You have to land it on the green.

Take more club and play the shot to the back of the green. As I have said before it's as easy putting from one side of the pin as from the other, so never be afraid of going past the pin. There may well be a bank at the rear of the green to help bring the ball back.

In the 1992 British Open at Muirfield, Nick Faldo did just that in hitting a wonderful 3-iron to the back of the last green.

The front of the green is protected by bunkers and it was into one of those that Paul Azinger had hit his approach a few years earlier, a shot that probably cost him the Open.

Faldo knew he could not afford to hit these bunkers so the shot that others might have played, running the ball into the front of the green, was not one of his options. He had only one thought in mind and that was to land the ball past the bunkers and on the green; if that meant going past the pin it was not a major problem as there was little trouble long.

That is exactly what he did, getting the ball to the back of the green to allow him to play it back to the pin and win the Open. That was a terrific shot, not only in its execution but in the thought processes that produced it.

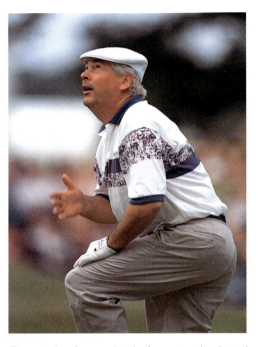

Be certain of your shot before you play it and only play those shots you have played before. The golf course is no place to be experimenting or hoping.

That is where he is so very good.

If you are playing to your handicap and have a stroke in hand, use it. Play to the fat of the green rather than possibly wasting it by going straight at the pin.

There is nothing wrong with taking a few shots on, but trust your own ability, rather than relying on Lady Luck.

Matchplay

Matchplay is different, because it does not matter how many strokes your opponent beats you by – you only lose that hole. Now you can have a go, but you must know how your opponent is lying. If he is on the green in three and you are playing two, go for the fat of the green rather than at the pin, because you will the be putting him under pressure to hole his putt, whilst you still have two. The extra pressure on him may unsettle him and you are sitting fairly comfortably.

If, however, the situation is reversed and he is on the fat of the green in two you may need to go for the pin, but as with that earlier shot to reach the green, make absolutely certain you have enough club to get there, safely carrying all the hazards.

It may also happen on the tee-shot, where your opponent hits a great drive down the middle, thus gaining a psychological advantage, and you think

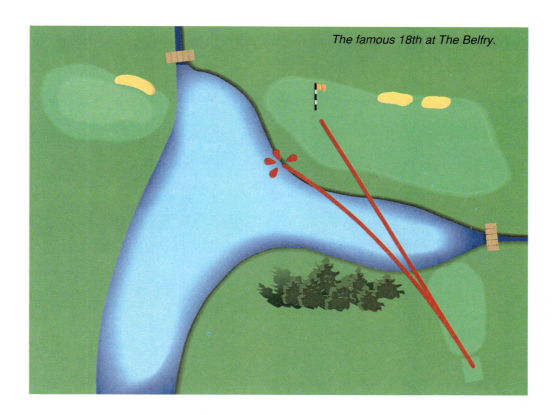

The famous 18th at The Belfry.

Playing from under trees requires extra care and attention if you are to keep the ball low yet achieve distance …

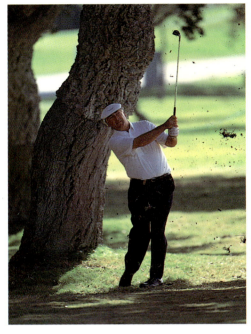

… as this shot at the 1992 British Masters shows. To keep the ball low I have cut off the follow-through, yet still hit the green.

you need to overtake him, with a view to leaving yourself with a second shot, to the green, shorter than his.

This happened so much in the 1989 Ryder Cup at The Belfry where, one after the other, a procession of Americans landed in the water down the left of the 18th. So many people came up to me later and asked how that happened.

They were trying just a little too hard to shorten that hole by keeping the ball further left and with the extra pressure they just slightly pulled it or bit off

more than they could chew. Yet there was not one badly hit drive among them, for they are all world-class players with great skill.

When you are hitting a drive to carry a hazard, allow yourself a good 20 yards extra safety margin. The ball should then run on into a safe area. If you can't safely carry the hazard, then lay up short of it.

Another example of being sure of your shots occurred to me in the British Masters at Woburn in 1992, which I was fortunate enough to win.

That shot led to a play-off and this putt ...

In the final round on the 16th I hit my drive to the right and it was under the trees. Tony Johnstone, with whom I was playing and who I went on to beat in a play-off, was on the green and I knew that if I just knocked the ball out onto the fairway I would almost inevitably take five, a dropped stroke which would have left me little chance of getting back.

Although there were a lot of press photographers in front of me, all of whom were expecting me to knock the ball out sideways, I saw the shot which would get me to the green.

There were overhanging branches so the ball had to be kept low but I also needed to fade the ball considerably to get it round the trees that were between the ball and the green.

When you keep a ball low it is easier to draw it, yet fading a ball low was a shot I had practised thousands of times so I knew I could do it. There was a need to keep it low because the ball rises much quicker than most people think. This time I was lucky and it stayed low and hit the green. It was a

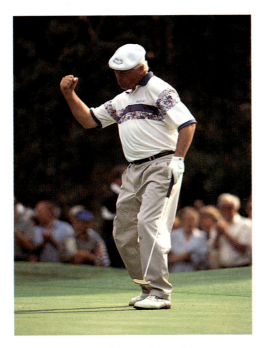

. . . which was celebrated like this . . .

. . . and led to this!

gamble but a shot I had played many, many times before. I had also 'seen' it clearly before hitting it.

At Valderrama later that year in the Volvo Masters virtually the same thing happened where I had to fade a ball 70 yards left to right to get round trees.

Again I hit it low and with a lot of cut, taking the club back well outside and coming straight across the ball. It, like all the other shots I have shown you in this book, is easy to hit if you will only take the time to go out to your local golf course, take a lesson or two from your club professional, going back to him regularly so that he can monitor your progress and iron out any faults in your game which appear from time to time, and then practise them.

All golf professionals spend time practising and although it is not your day job to play golf, if you really want to improve you must spend time on the practice range.

Always warm up first, hitting the shorter clubs to begin with until you have a smooth rhythm going and your muscles are moving nicely.

Give yourself some variety, shaping your shots from time to time rather than just trying to hit draw after draw. Hit some high, some low, fade some and draw some.

Hit to different distances too, rather than just attacking one position. If you can have a definite target in view it will help you – a flag, perhaps or, if none is available, walk down the range and stick an umbrella in the ground at about 140 yards.

Hit to it, short of it and just past it, trying to get the ball to do what you want it to do.

Use different clubs for the same distances rather than just going up or down a club. Learning to run the ball or to pitch it high with a club you might not normally use for that distance will help you understand better the value if each club and what you can do with it.

Work your way gradually up to the woods, hitting some drives and, as I have suggested earlier, hitting some shots with the driver off the fairway without a tee-peg.

Before you leave the practice ground work on your short game and on bunkers, giving yourself some awkward lies that you need to recover from, rather than having a perfect lie every time. Believe me, you're never that lucky on the golf course.

And of course, don't forget the putting practice, for that is half the

Hit through the ball every time. The club does the work.

game of golf. Practise putting to different distances, sending just two balls to each target rather than hitting ball after ball to the same target.

Before I say goodbye a couple of words about your clubs and then a few reminders of things we have looked at.

Then I'll wish you well and hope that you enjoy your golf as much as I have done over the many years since I began playing.

Club Care

I began this book by telling you to get to know your golf clubs. Now I am going to tell you how to look after them, for so often I see poorly kept clubs.

You should clean the grooves out regularly, making sure, before each shot, that the clubface is clean and free of grass and dirt. If you have grass on the clubface it will stop you hitting a perfect shot.

Look after your clubs and they will look after you.

I know I have a caddy to help me but it is really easy to have a damp towel on the golf bag and to wipe the club clean after you have taken your shot. Your club professional can regroove the clubs after a while, making sure you continue to get as good a shot from them as when they were brand new.

Also clean your golf ball between holes and, if it has mud or sand on it, on the green before you putt, as a little mud on one side of the ball can throw your putt off line quite easily. We change our ball every few holes in a tournament but the surlyn balls you will probably use don't cut like the balata balls we use.

I really think you should have head covers for your woods, whether wooden or metal. They do protect them and keep them in good condition.

A good wood should last up to 20 years and, if looked after, will, but you will need a head cover. The shaft may weaken after a while but your club professional has a machine which can test the frequency of the shaft and it can be replaced. He can also replace the grips, making sure the size grip you have fits your hands.

I see so many worn grips on the golf course, with the grip being shiny with no adhesion possible. Get them replaced as it only costs a very little in comparison to the set of clubs.

SOME REMINDERS

The Driver

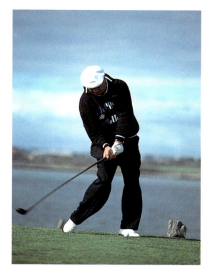

Fairway Woods

A Long Iron Draw

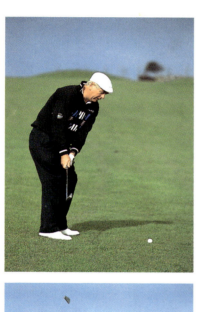

Bunkers

A Short Chip